Wilhelm Friedrich Besser, Friedrich Bultmann

**St. Paul the Apostle**

A Biblical Portrait and a Mirror of the Manifold Grace of God

Wilhelm Friedrich Besser, Friedrich Bultmann

**St. Paul the Apostle**
*A Biblical Portrait and a Mirror of the Manifold Grace of God*

ISBN/EAN: 9783337156206

Printed in Europe, USA, Canada, Australia, Japan

Cover: Foto ©Lupo / pixelio.de

More available books at **www.hansebooks.com**

# ST PAUL THE APOSTLE:

## A BIBLICAL PORTRAIT

AND

## A MIRROR OF THE MANIFOLD GRACE OF GOD.

BY

W. F. BESSER, D.D.

TRANSLATED BY

FREDERIC BULTMANN,
MISSIONARY OF THE CHURCH MISSIONARY SOCIETY.

WITH AN INTRODUCTORY NOTICE BY
REV. J. S. HOWSON, D.D.

NEW YORK:
ROBERT CARTER & BROTHERS,
No. 530 BROADWAY.
1864.

# INTRODUCTORY NOTICE.

DURING the last ten or twenty years a very remarkable attention has been given, in many countries, to the study of the Life and Personal Character of St Paul. A large number of books might be mentioned, published during this period, on the whole or on part of this subject, in England and Germany, Holland and France. Among these books, the small volume here presented to the reader deserves to hold a conspicuous place.

My share in the publication of this translation has been limited to making arrangements with the publisher, to correcting the proof-sheets, and giving a more English turn to some of the sentences which seemed to require it. In discharging the last of these tasks, I have confined myself within narrow bounds, and most scrupulously avoided communicating the least shade of difference of meaning to any single expression. Sometimes I have fancied that the translator did not exhibit quite exactly the author's thought; but in such cases I have not felt myself at liberty (and, indeed, with my inadequate knowledge of German, it would have been presumptuous) to make any changes in the sense. My difficulty was further increased by the fact that I have had simply the published edition of Dr Besser's "Paulus" before me, whereas Mr Bultmann (as he says in his preface) executed his translation within reach of notes prepared by the author for a second edition : and in some cases I see that the variation is considerable. These explanations will doubtless be thought sufficient, if the whole book is found to wear, as regards its phraseology, a German complexion, if some parts are rather obscure, and others contain expressions and images which seem strange to the English reader. When an author writes somewhat quaintly in his own language, it is difficult to preserve this characteristic in a translation.

My own work and responsibility in this instance having been so light, it seems hardly necessary to say more. I may just add, however, that in certain details I do not agree with the author's views. Thus I think very great objections lie against his opinion that the First Epistle to Timothy and the Epistle to Titus were written during the residence at Ephesus, described in the nineteenth chapter of the Acts. All serious difficulties in regard to these epistles vanish if we retain the old opinion, that the Apostle was liberated from the Roman imprisonment recorded at the end of that book. And Dr Besser himself, in common with a large number of the most recent writers, quite accepts that well-supported view.* On the other hand, while differing sometimes in circumstantial detail, it is a great pleasure to me to express my hearty concurrence in the general delineation here given of the Apostle's character. Thus (to mention one point, which has not always been very distinctly noticed in connexion with the sequence of the events of St Paul's life) I see that Dr Besser has been struck, as I was† before reading his book, with the peculiarly elastic and joyous tone of the epistles written during that very imprisonment, after a time of much depression, suffering, and trial.

One other subject calls for a single remark. Mr Bultmann has thought it desirable to state that he does not quite accord with Dr Besser's somewhat "High-Church views." It does not appear to me necessary to lay peculiar stress on this point. It may be of service to some Eng-

\* Some English Churchmen would not be satisfied with what is said on Church Order in the last chapter: but the author virtually admits that the germ of Episcopacy was planted in the missions of Timothy and Titus; and the argument hence derived is not touched by the fact that the words "bishop" and "presbyter" are convertible in Acts xx. 17, 28, and Tit. i. 5, 7.

† I may take the liberty of referring here to p. 208 (second edition) of the "Hulsean Lectures for 1862: Five Lectures on the Character of St Paul, by J. S. Howson, D.D."

lish readers to see how a German, who holds the doctrine of Justification by Faith in the purest and strictest sense, yet looks on Baptism as the entrance to great spiritual blessings, believes that the Lord's Supper is a means of grace of the utmost moment, and sets a high value on the external unity of the Church. Our own Ecclesiastical and Sacramental controversies have separated us from one another; and it may be well that those who have been so divided should at last draw more closely together. Worse dangers now surround us than any which are connected with such disputes. As regards the Supernatural character of Christianity, the Redemption wrought for us by Christ, and the reverence due to the Holy Scriptures, Dr Besser will be found unfaltering. His "Paulus" is a popular book as opposed to a mere theological treatise; but it is evidently based on a careful, minute, and prolonged study of all that is said in the New Testament by St Paul, and of St Paul; and I believe it will be found full of useful suggestions to those whose duty it is to teach others, as well as eminently adapted to build up unlearned believers "in their most holy faith."

J. S. H.

LIVERPOOL, *Feb.* 2, 1864.

TO

### THE REV. H. VENN, B.D.,

PREBENDARY OF ST PAUL'S, HON. SEC. OF THE CHURCH MISSIONARY SOCIETY,

## This "Portrait"

OF THE FIRST GREAT MISSIONARY

IS,

IN GRATEFUL REMEMBRANCE OF THE MANY KINDNESSES

EXPERIENCED DURING A MISSIONARY SERVICE OF TWENTY-THREE YEARS

UNDER THE CHURCH MISSIONARY SOCIETY,

RESPECTFULLY INSCRIBED BY

THE TRANSLATOR.

# PREFACE.

"Exempla trahunt,"—"Examples draw." To a nation so fond as the English of drawing by example, and so successful in it, that their works of this description are admired and copied by other nations, it is hoped that this "Portrait," drawn by a fond hand, of the man to whom, under God, we are all indebted for untold blessings, will not be unacceptable.

How this first Apostle of the Gentiles—Saint Paul, chosen for the work from his mother's womb—was called and prepared for it by Divine grace,—how he laboured and suffered, and was blessed in it through Divine grace,—in short, how he lived and died a monument of God's grace in Christ Jesus, and how in the rich legacy of his word and work he has bequeathed to the Church of all ages a fund of inexhaustible blessings,—these are the main features of this biographical sketch, drawn in vivid colours by the author's masterly hand.

Among his "Biblical Portraits" that of Saint Paul is by far the richest; nor would he proceed to draw it, until—in his deservedly popular "Bibelstunden,"* ("Bible Les-

---

* Animated by the author's encouragement to it, and having every reason to hope that they will be as acceptable to the English, as they are

sons," all of which, before publication, he personally delivered to his flock,)—he had gone through the Acts and Romans, in both which, to use (with him) an expression of Gregory of Nazianzum, he found "what Paul saith of Paul." "And now I am bold to say," he adds, "that I come with full hands; for they have been filled by the word of the Spirit, who has drawn after life the picture of the wonderful man, whom to draw after Him has been my delight."

It has appeared proper to the author, and rightly so, first, to complete the historical picture of his hero, (Chapters I.-VI.,) in order, in the last four Chapters, (VII.-X.,) to concentrate again all the sparks of light thus gathered, in "the Man of Faith," and "of Hope," and "of Love;" and then, finally, to sum up all in "the Man of the Church." If any should think that the author's partiality for this man of God has carried his praise and admiration of him beyond proper bounds, let him remember Christ's word: "*I am glorified in them.*" It was in this light only—under the constant deep sense of glorifying the Redeemer in the redeemed—that the author could venture, and has ventured, to dip his pen so deeply into praise, and to draw in such glowing colours the picture of the man who has said of himself, "By the grace of God I am what I am."

One remark, however, I dare not shrink from making here. The author being one of those strict Lutherans who, for conscience' sake, separated from the National Church of Prussia,* the reader will here and there meet with—no

fondly cherished by the German Bible-reader, I shall (D.V.) prepare an edition of them for the English public.

\* By a Royal Act of Uniformity, passed in 1830, the two Protestant sections of the National Church—Lutheran and Reformed—were fused

Tractarian, but—somewhat "High-Church views," though "no higher," he declares, "than the Church herself, the Bride of the Lamb." And as an "Evangelical" Churchman myself, identified—through many years' service under it—with the principles of the Church Missionary Society, I feel no hesitation in assuring the "Evangelical" reader, that he will not peruse these pages (nor any of Dr Besser's works) without conceiving the highest regard for the author, and, I may confidently add, without blessing him for the many precious pearls and rich thoughts of wholesome doctrine they contain. Indeed, I am acquainted with no writer of my country better calculated to redeem the honour of our German theology, and take away much of the prejudice so generally felt against it by the "evangelical party" in England. For in no page of Dr Besser's pen will they ever find the least unsoundness in doctrine, much less any taint of "rationalism;" which, on the contrary, at every fitting occasion, is crushingly handled

---

into one, thenceforth called "The United (*Unirte*) Church of Prussia." Upon the introduction of a modified Liturgy (*Agende*) to suit both parties, the author refused to acknowledge "its right," and declined accepting a dispensation from its use under condition of making that acknowledgment. Being thence removed from office (in the "United" Church) in 1847, (which he had held since 1841,) he ministered for some years to a Nonconformist congregation at "Seefeld," whence he was called to act as "Co-director of the Lutheran Missionary Society" at Leipzig, until, in 1857, he accepted, at great sacrifice, the unanimous call of a poor Lutheran congregation at Waldenburg, in Silesia, of which he is still the pastor.

In a recent translation of his "Gospel of St John," published by Messrs T. & T. Clark of Edinburgh, the translator, a Mrs Huxtable, has mistaken the author for his cousin, "Rudolph" Besser, the well-known publisher of Gotha; an error which, at his request, I take this opportunity of correcting. Dr Besser's name is "Wilhelm Friedrich."

by him with the weapons and in the spirit of his great exemplar—Saint Paul, the servant of Jesus Christ.

Hardly two years have elapsed since the appearance of Dr Besser's "Paulus," (Leipzig, 1861,) and now another edition is called for, with the notes prepared for which the author has kindly furnished me for the present translation. At his request, I have the pleasure of expressing his indebtedness to "The Life and Epistles of St Paul," by W. J. Conybeare and J. S. Howson, (London, 1853.) Nor can I forbear to join my own thanks, with those of the author, to the Rev. Dr Howson, Principal of the Collegiate Institution, Liverpool, for his very kind exertions to secure a publisher for this little work, which Dr Besser owns to be the "darling" among his "literary children." And, finally, our joint prayer is, that many readers may be incited by the perusal of these pages to become the followers of Paul, even as he was of Christ.

F. BULTMANN.

OLDENBURG, 31st Oct. 1863.

# CONTENTS.

|  |  | PAGE |
|---|---|---|
| I. | THE CHOSEN VESSEL, | 1 |
| II. | THE PHARISEE, | 14 |
| III. | THE PERSECUTOR, | 23 |
| IV. | THE WON OF THE LORD JESUS, | 33 |
| V. | THE LABOURER, | 44 |
| VI. | THE PRISONER OF JESUS CHRIST, | 71 |
| VII. | THE MAN OF FAITH, | 98 |
| VIII. | THE MAN OF HOPE, | 124 |
| IX. | THE MAN OF LOVE, | 152 |
| X. | THE MAN OF THE CHURCH, | 184 |

# I.

## THE CHOSEN VESSEL.

*" God separated me from my mother's womb, and called me by his grace."*
—GAL. i. 15.

ST PAUL laboured more than all the apostles, but also wearied the Lord more with his sins, and is himself a masterpiece of that divine grace, the exceeding riches of which he preached and extolled more than any of them. Yea, it is *what he was in* Christ which gives that peculiar soul-winning attraction to his *preaching of* Christ. Upon the shoulders of this Israelite of the tribe of Benjamin, " the beloved of the Lord," rests the loveliness of the Lord, (Deut. xxxiii. 12,) viz., the Church gathered from among the Gentiles and become " the Israel of God ;" and as in her the manifold wisdom of God is made known unto principalities and powers in heavenly places, (Eph. iii. 10,) so the manifold lustre of the grace of Christ is reflected in the instrument He chose for effecting that blessed end. St Paul does not stand by the side of the twelve apostles as the thirteenth, but as the one to whom, though last called, the mystery of the embodying of the Gentiles into the Church of Christ—as "the Israel of God," (Gal. vi. 16,)—was made known first, even before St Peter. And when we read of St John seeing the names of the twelve apostles of the Lamb engraven in the twelve foundations of the new Jerusalem, (Rev. xxi. 14,) this twelve-fold splendour, we might almost say, is reflected in the one great apostle of the Gentiles, who, by the very discharge of his high commission—to bring the Gentiles to the obedience of the faith—became, as it were, a saving angel also to his own brethren after the flesh, by inciting them to emulation, as the last means of restoring the remnant of that fallen race to the true Israel of God, (Rom. ix. 27, xi. 5, 14.)* Could life-portraits be drawn of the apostles and other eminent servants of God, St Paul's certainly would be one of the richest, and would shine resplendent in a picture gallery of biblical characters. Yea, and were we to single out one of the many precious jewels shining in the Redeemer's crown, St Paul would be that jewel, for in this "chosen vessel" the Holy Spirit has caused to shine with special lustre the image of Christ, (2 Cor. iii. 18.) In him we hear the opposite of "sounding brass," or "tinkling cymbal," his whole character and life being the sweetest melody to the theme of his apostolical teaching.

Let us now, with humble thankfulness to the Giver of all grace, contemplate the character of this "chosen vessel," through whom Christ has bequeathed to His Church a rich store of imperishable blessings, from which thousands in all ages have drawn for their souls treasures of unspeakable worth; which, however, will be appreciated by us only in proportion as we desire to become followers of him, "as he was of Christ."

"By God's grace I am what I am," says the apostle, (1 Cor. xv. 10,) and therewith looks back from the height of his apostolical career through all the wonderful ways God had led him, down to the very "hole of the pit whence he was digged." For what does he mean by God having separated and called him by His grace? Surely he would not have us infer from it, that God had done so, because

* A further explanation of this—and especially the word "last"—the reader may expect in the author's peculiar interpretation of Rom. xi.—TR.

He foresaw what hereafter would become of him. No, God's prescience is never an idle, always an *effective* knowledge. " Thou hast possessed my reins," prays David; "thou hast covered me in my mother's womb," (Ps. cxxxix. 13.) So with regard to this " chosen vessel "—the Israelite Saul of Benjamin's tribe,—God from his mother's womb effectively separated and called him unto that definite end for which His grace was to fit him in time. His natural endowments, his talents, his temperament, the tone and disposition of his character, his frailty of body and strength of soul, his very birthplace, society and education: all these, and a thousand other things, were not foreknown only by God—for " known unto Him are all His works," —but His guiding hand so directed and disposed them all, as best to magnify in and through this " chosen vessel " the abundant riches of His mercy and grace in Christ.

Twice the apostle mentions his descent from the tribe of Benjamin, (Rom. xi. 1; Phil. iii. 5.) Besides this we find hardly any distinction by tribe mentioned in the New Testament. With the exception of Elizabeth, the daughter of Aaron, (Luke i. 4,) in whose son Levi found his greatest representative, (Matt. xi. 11,) and above all Mary, of the house of David, (Luke i. 27,) in whose son Judah found his Shiloh, (Gen. xlix. 10; Rev. v. 5,) we only find two persons mentioned by their tribe—Anna a prophetess of the tribe of Aser, (Luke ii. 36,) and Barnabas a Levite of Cyprus, (Acts iv. 36.) Not one even of the twelve apostles is distinguished by his tribe. No doubt Paul had studied the history of his own with special care and interest, nor can we help tracing in it some significant parallels to his own life. A Benoni (" son of sorrows") Saul also was, and became a Benjamin, (" son of my right hand,") on finding his heavenly Joseph, whom—like the patriarch his brother—he met away from Israel, in a heathen land. The warlike propensity of this tribe, borne from Jacob's blessing, (Gen. xlix. 27,) through the generations of Israel, was to find, as it were, its consummation in him. For as Saul, the Benjamite of old, persecuted David of Judah, (whose reign, nevertheless, he could not prevent,) so this new Saul persecuted the son of David, till—the bow of his native strength being broken—he swore allegiance to "the Lion of the tribe of Juda," and henceforth fought manfully under His banner, enduring hardness as a good soldier " of Christ."

St Paul's family seems to have been scattered through heathen lands : Macedonia, Greece and Rome, (cf. Rom. xvi. 7, 11, 22.) He himself, we know, was a native of Tarsus in Cilicia, and he inherited from his father the freedom of a Roman citizen, (Acts xxi. 39, xxii. 28.) Yet not Rome, but Jerusalem was the pride of his family. Where he calls to remembrance Timothy's blessing, as inherited from his pious mother and grandmother, there he makes mention also of his own devout forefathers, from whom he served God with a pure conscience, (2 Tim. i. 3.) Thus we find young Saul growing up in the bosom of a family, outwardly indeed the citizens of heathen Rome, but inwardly clinging to the land of their fathers, and doubtless the more eagerly longing for the Hope of their nation, since she was doomed still to dwell among the heathen, where she found no rest, (Lam. i. 3.)

Israel's King and Saviour had already appeared, when young Saul was still learning of his parents to sigh with the prophet: "Watchman, what of the night?" For to Tarsus the fame of the great Prophet, in whom God had visited His people, had most likely not reached ere young Saul left it for Jerusalem; where, however, he may have already been living, probably in the house of his married sister, (Acts xxiii. 16,) at the time when, amid loud hosannas, Zion's King entered that city, and when, but a few days after, Zion's Saviour was led as a lamb to the slaughter. Nor could he help hearing of what set all Jerusalem in commotion, (Luke xxiv. 18;) but seeking, as then he was, his own righteousness, and learning from his teachers, the Pharisees, that "this man" was "a sinner," he might scorn to run along with the multitude in order to see Him. Some of his kinsmen—Andronicus and Junia —we know "were in Christ before" him, and so was the wife of Simon (the cross-bearer) of Cyrene, the mother of his friend Rufus, for she also became his mother in the Lord, (Rom. xvi. 7, 13.) But Saul, separated from his mother's womb, long resisted the drawings of divine grace, scorning in pharisaic righteousness the very thought of a crucified Saviour for sinners. And yet the Lord was already preparing His chosen vessel in this proud youth of Benjamin.

A religious sense—that tie of the human heart to God —was ever strong in Saul, though as yet he was, in misbelief, pursuing a phantom of his own creation. It was the misconceived notion of Israel's return to righteousness, and thence to merited glory and perpetual reign under the promised son of David, which formed the centre of all his hopes and aims, so long as, in ignorance of God's righteousness by faith in Christ, he went about to establish his own by the works of the law. It has often been remarked, that Saul possessed all the natural requisites for becoming what the world calls a "great man." And true it is, by the energy of his will, and the uncommon quickness of his thought, he would have made an excellent commander; or a poet, by the depth and tenderness of his feeling; or a philosopher, by the acuteness of his subtle reasonings; or a statesman, by his discernment of men and his masterly method of order. The same Lord who called unlearned

fishermen and publicans to be apostles, (in accordance with
1 Cor. i. 26–29,) fitted this future apostle of the Gentiles with
a fulness of natural gifts rarely equalled, to make him, as it
were, a silver vessel for the golden contents of His grace.

One striking feature in his being separated from the
womb for God's service was the early and constant bent of
his life toward Jerusalem, his people's glory. Though as
yet he knew not the free Jerusalem which is above, yet his
Jewish patriotism would make him enter heart and soul
into Israel's song of Zion : " If I forget thee, O Jerusalem !
let my right hand forget her cunning. If I do not remember thee, let my tongue cleave to the roof of my mouth; if
I prefer not Jerusalem above my chief joy," (Ps. cxxxvii.)
To establish Israel's righteousness after the law, and with
his people to witness Jerusalem's prosperity, was all the
bent of his strong mind, of the granite-like constancy of his
character. There was no difficulty from which he would
shrink, no wall he would not attempt to climb; and foiled
ever so often, he would return to the struggle and labour
on. His tenderest feelings of sympathy—afterwards en-
nobled into love—were excited by the wretched degrada-
tion of his down-trodden nation. It was, as it were, the
time of Israel's widowhood ; and in his willing celibacy he
felt as though he were betrothed to her, and his life devoted
to her service. All the riches of his mind,—his rare talent
for making deductions and logically resolving a subject
into its parts, unfolding the rich meaning of a single word,
and studding, as it were, out of one germ, a whole meadow
with flowers, the ingenious, yea, fountain-like originality
wherewith thought after thought seems to issue forth from
one fundamental idea, around which all range themselves
in order, like the circumference of a circle around its centre,
his pointed wit, too, and his charming grace,—in fine, all
his talents and powers of mind centered in this one object :

Israel's restoration to her pristine glory, by a return to her national righteousness after the law, as the condition laid down in Moses and the Prophets,—in a word, to see all the gracious thoughts of the God of his fathers realised concerning His people. Nor were his energies, wrongly directed as now they were, exerted in vain; for they served to prepare for his high office the future herald of Christ's righteousness. All the munition of legal learning which now he brought into the field against Christ was hereafter to be turned into a crushing weapon against pharisaic Judaism.

From Acts xxii. 3, we know that young Saul was brought up and taught according to the "perfect manner of the law" by one Gamaliel, a Pharisee, and doctor of the law, held in reputation among all the people, and who is presented to us by St Luke, (Acts v. 34, &c.,) in the favourable light of shielding the apostles' lives by his equitable advocacy in their behalf, thus shewing him to have been a very different man from the worldly, persecuting Sadducees, (ib. ver. 17,) from whose infidel tenets he would turn with disgust, far as he himself might be from seeking the hope of Israel in a crucified and risen Redeemer. The wonders wrought in Solomon's porch by the hands of the apostles, (ib. ver. 12–16,) and Peter's bold defence and testimony of Christ before the Council, (ib. ver. 29–32,) could not, indeed, fail to bring the question home to his heart, whether this work might not be of God, (ib. ver. 39;) but, like a true Pharisee, he would look for the kingdom of God to come "with observation," (Luke xvii. 20,) and therefore probably expect, that if this Jesus whom Peter preached to be "a Prince and a Saviour," were indeed the promised Messiah, God would shew Him (as such) openly on Mount Sion, and lay all the heathen prostrate at His feet. With what eagerness may young Saul have listened to this honourable Pharisee! and how, sitting at his feet, would all his attention be absorbed in his arguments, as he might seek to demonstrate out of Moses and the Prophets the character of their still-longed-for Messiah, sitting upon the throne of David, awarding eternal life to His chosen people, the heathen and uttermost parts of the earth His possession, Israel's laws those of the world, and Jerusalem's temple a house of prayer for all people! How would Saul's youthful soul, thirsting for the glory of Israel, revel in prospects like these! and how, under such transporting thoughts, would his ire be stirred, when he heard one of the despised sect of the Nazarene tear to pieces, by his spirited arguments, all these carnal hopes of the Pharisees, who, unable to resist the wisdom and spirit by which he spake, suborned men, accusing him of "blasphemous words against Moses and against God," (Acts vi. 10, 11.) Yet Saul was soon to become heir to both the wisdom and spirit of this faithful confessor; and we have to look upon his meeting with St Stephen as, under God's providence, one of the most powerful demonstrations of that grace which was already seeking his soul, though he knew it not.

Gamaliel's teaching, however, of Jewish law and divinity, was not the limit of Saul's education; he was trained, moreover, from his youth in Grecian knowledge and wisdom. When yet a boy in his native town of Tarsus he had already the opportunity of hearing those that were masters in Hellenic art, rhetoric and philosophy. Strabo, in speaking of the inhabitants of that famous city, says that they displayed such zeal in philosophy and all branches of general science, that they excelled those of all other towns, not even excepting Athens and Alexandria. Though designed for a rabbi, Saul, according to Jewish custom, also learned a handicraft—that of tent-maker, (Acts xviii. 3.) Still he found time for learned studies. As he read the Greek poets and philosophers, (cf. Acts xvii. 28; Tit. i. 12,) and as he followed the winding ways in which their heathen minds sought after the unknown God, if haply they might feel after and find Him;—as he gained insight into the history of their deep fall into spiritual and moral depravity, into their outward splendour and inner wretchedness;—as he was led to contemplate the goodness of God, both in His judgments and preservation of them;—as he made himself master of the language then spoken by all the learned in the whole world, and in which human genius has woven its finest and richest garment,—Saul knew not to whose service all this acquisition of knowledge was destined to be devoted; that even this training also belonged to the separation from his mother's womb for the service of Christ among the Gentiles—"For all things serve thee," (Ps. cxix. 91.) The Holy Ghost, by whom "holy men of God are moved" to speak and act, despises not to make use of all the powers of the human mind, after He has purified and consecrated them. To the picture of the man who preached and "taught publicly, and from house to house," who was "instant in season and out of season," who "ceased not to warn every one night and day with tears," and who, beside that which came upon him daily—"the care of all the churches," yet ministered with his hands unto his own necessities and those that were with him;—to the picture of that man, also, belongs this trait, that amid all his labours he still continued to study and to read, even requesting Timothy, in the very last epistle he wrote—when already brought before Nero the second time—to bring him "the books and parchments" which he had left at Troas, (2 Tim. iv. 13.)

Yet, taught by grace, how little did this great man think of himself! To the Corinthians he writes: "Of myself I will not glory, but in mine infirmities," (2 Cor. xii. 5.)

He knew that he had nothing which he had not received, (1 Cor. iv. 7.) His greatest privileges by birth and advantages by nature, all these he counted but "loss," yea, but "dung" for the "excellency of the knowledge of Christ Jesus" his Lord, (Phil. iii. 4, &c.) Not the strength he had inherited from his mother's womb, but his very weakness he looked upon as a preparatory grace of Him that called him. And a twofold weakness this was. As an adherent of the "straitest sect of Jews," (Acts xxvi. 5,) he was made to experience, under the burden of the law, that weakness of which he speaks, (Rom. v. 6,) "For when we were yet without strength, in due time Christ died for us." But of this weakness, which he was deeply to experience under grace's training, we shall come to speak in the next chapter—Saul "the Pharisee." Here we shall speak of that "weakness" and those "infirmities," of which he says, "Most gladly, therefore, will I rather glory in them, that the power of Christ may rest upon me," (2 Cor. xii. 9.) What he means by the "thorn in the flesh," (v. 7,) which he had to carry about with him, "the messenger of Satan" to buffet him, (after the manner of Job,) he has wisely withheld from us, not unlikely for this obvious reason, that *every* Christian, suffering under whatsoever temptation, might have the benefit of applying to his own peculiar case the ghostly comfort to be derived from this doleful apostolic confession. Far from rejecting Luther's view of the apostle alluding to some "great spiritual temptation," yet we deem it more than likely that Satan, as his basis for buffeting him, had recourse to some grievous bodily affliction,—a view which seems clearly indicated by many allusions we find in his Epistles. "Through infirmity of the flesh" he preached the gospel to the Galatians, and he praises them for not having despised or taken offence at his "temptation which was in the flesh,"

(Gal. iv. 13, 14.) His proud opponents at Corinth, he hears say of him: "His letters are weighty and powerful, but his bodily presence is weak, and his speech contemptible," (2 Cor. x. 10; cf. v. 1: "who in presence am base among you.") Thus, it should seem, we have to think of the apostle as in his person weak and infirm; and as such Raphael has also painted him. "A poor, lean, little man, like Master Philip," (Melancthon,) so Luther thought of him; and Nicophorus Callisti, an Oriental Church historian of the fourteenth century, also calls him "a short, stooping man." Nor is it improbable, that his first acquaintance with Luke was as his "beloved physician;" and Phœbe's succour and Mary's labour (Rom. xvi. 2, 6) may likewise have been bestowed on his bodily infirmities. But why does he glory in such his infirmities? Because he was thereby drawn to cast himself entirely into the arms of his heavenly Lord. If we read the register of his labours and sufferings, which, in sorrow to be compelled to such "foolish boasting," he details in 2 Cor. xi.; if we hear him relate to the elders of the Ephesian church at Miletus in what manner he had been with them at all seasons, (Acts xx. 17, &c.;) if we follow his whole course from Jerusalem to Rome, as St Luke has penned it, and add to it the entire train of sacrifices his Epistles develop, truly a gigantic strength would seem to have been requisite for undergoing all that labour—all those sufferings! But, behold, his body was feeble! "I can do all things through Christ which strengtheneth me," (Phil. iv. 13.) To make this precious truth the more deeply felt, it was to this end that he inherited such weakness from his mother's womb. By the power of Christ alone he would allow himself to be borne, (2 Cor. iv. 10,) learning thus to express the mystery of his strength: "When I am weak, then am I strong," (2 Cor. xii. 10.) With this view even the frail body of this chosen vessel was formed; and right well was proved and exemplified in Paul what the blessed Woltersdorf sings of his own experience :—

> "And though it go through weakness e'er so sad,
> I follow, at His call, my heavenly guide;
> The work which does but rest on Christ my head,
> Despite my impotence, must sure abide.
> When sick are both the body and the soul,
> We see that Jesus only does the whole."

From the above-quoted taunt of his adversaries at Corinth, "his speech is contemptible," it would appear that the apostle had some defect in his tongue, which hindered him from becoming what the world calls a "good speaker;" and, indeed, he himself says : "Though I be rude in speech, [literally, a lay-speaker,] yet not in knowledge; but we have been thoroughly made manifest among you in all things," (2 Cor. xi. 6.) Strange! Paul no speaker. And certainly Apollos better pleased the ticklish ears of the Corinthians; and the Athenians, whose ears were still more spoiled, called him a "babbler," (Acts xvii. 18,) enough to shew that he had not the best natural organ of speech. A strong, and often violent struggle with language which he forces into the expression of divine thoughts, is his idiom. While "casting down imaginations, and every high thing that exalteth itself against the knowledge of God, and bringing into captivity every thought to the obedience of Christ," (2 Cor. x. 5,) he could not bring to his aid the carnal weapons of a powerful organ, a modulation of voice, or an imposing person. But what his all-prevailing weapon was, he tells us in 1 Cor. ii. 4; it consisted in "demonstration of the Spirit and of power." Not any "excellency of speech or of wisdom," but solely the things he preached, the spirit in which he preached them, and the fulness of life out of which he drew them : this was what attracted men's hearts, and drew so many souls to Christ. Demosthenes, the great orator of Greece, forced his heavy tongue, by persevering efforts, into suppleness and eloquence; but Paul, like Moses, "of a slow tongue," painted, in "contemptible speech," before all men's eyes, Him who had "no form nor comeliness," and yet was "fairer than the children of men," and "full of grace in His lips." Tertullus, the Roman orator, (Acts xxiv. 1, &c.,) no doubt surpassed Paul in rhetorical art, yet how undauntedly does the apostle open his mouth before Jews and Gentiles, high priests and kings, in his weakness leaning upon Him who hath said, "I will give you a mouth and wisdom, which all your adversaries shall not be able to gainsay nor resist," (Luke xxi. 15.)

Thus strength and weakness both were made to serve in making this "chosen vessel" of the Lord what through grace he became.

> "Though separated from his mother's womb,
> And chose a vessel meet for heav'nly use,
> Paul, that his nature might to grace succumb,
> Was led through bitter ways man would not choose;
> For first must die in him the man called Saul,
> That grace supreme might live and reign in Paul."

## II.

### THE PHARISEE.

*"I was alive without the law once; but when the commandment came, sin revived."*—ROM. vii. 9.

SUCH a Pharisee as the man in Luke xviii. 11, satisfied in his negative righteousness, Saul was not. No, he took bitter pains in his Pharisaism, walking, as he was taught, according to the perfect manner of the law of the fathers, being zealous toward God, (Acts xxii. 3;) and he painfully felt the rod of the legal driver, when, ignorant of God's righteousness, he went about to establish his own, (Rom. x. 3.) The star of his hope, the glorious splendour of Messiah's reign, he could conceive only as rising over "a righteous nation which keepeth the truth," or "the faith," (as Luther has rendered Is. xxvi. 2.) To keep the faith was all Saul's aim; but he knew not what faith is, though we have learnt it of Paul to be no human work nor virtue, but that organ wrought in our heart through God's word and Spirit, by means of which we apprehend and receive with childlike trust and confidence, the riches of His grace in Christ Jesus our Lord. But to Saul the Pharisee it still was a work, a legal virtue, the due respect and literal observance of all God-appointed institutions and ordinances, circumcision, the passover, and the reading of the Law and the Prophets on every Sabbath; all which he kept strictly, and walked in unblamably. "Prepare ye the way of the Lord!" This prophetic call to repentance would sound in Saul's ear as a spur to unremitting exertions; for not till his nation should have returned to unblamable righteousness could he think that Messiah would appear to deliver Israel from all her enemies, and crown His chosen people with glory and honour in His kingdom of righteousness. These were the cravings of Saul's soul.

"Touching the righteousness which is in the law, blameless," (Phil. iii. 6,) this was his motto as a Pharisee. Before men he had succeeded in obtaining this blamelessness, and to obtain it before God did not appear to him out of the reach of his power. For how should God have given laws to His people which they were not able to keep? Righteousness, then, must verily be obtainable by the deeds of the law, which must give life, or else it were not "holy and just, and good." So Saul argued and thought. Had he been a hypocritical, or even superficial Pharisee, the coming to a compromise with the requirements of the law might have caused him little difficulty. But he felt the deadly point of the law in the tenth commandment, "Thou shalt not covet," (Rom. vii. 7;) and the knowledge of its spirituality discovered to him that he was "carnal, sold under sin," (Rom. vii. 14.)* But did this discovery make

* Like that honest farmer (Michael was his name) who, on his death-bed, called out to his son: "Jack, just reach down the Catechism from yonder shelf, to see how my past life agrees with it. Please, read me the commandments." "Thou shalt have none other gods but me. Thou shalt not make to thyself any graven image," &c. "Oh, these two I have always kept; I have neither worshipped idols, like the heathen, nor bowed down to images, like the Roman Catholics. Please, proceed to the third." "Thou shalt not take the name of the Lord thy God in vain," &c. "Here I am right also; I never swore an oath except in a court of justice; pray, pass to the next." "Remember that thou keep holy the Sabbath-day." "Oh, there I am not to blame either; I have always gone to church of a Sunday, and never played at cards, nor made my servants work. Which follows now?" "Honour thy father and thy mother." "Ay, as to that, Jack, I may well bid you follow my example; for when a boy I shewed

Saul lose trust in his own power? By no means; it incited him only the more earnestly to set about establishing his own righteousness. "And I profited," he says, "in the Jews' religion above many mine equals in mine own nation, being more exceedingly zealous of the traditions of my fathers," (Gal. i. 14.) He knew only one way of silencing his conscience, which accused him of the lust stirred up in his members by the commandment; and that was, by keeping the commandment. Even that chiefest of all: "Thou shalt love the Lord thy God with all thine heart, and with all thy soul, and with all thy might," (Deut. vi. 5,) he despaired not to attain to it, and therefore entered his resolute "No" to the death-threatening sentence of the law. He knew nothing yet of the law "working death" in him, "that sin by the commandment might become exceeding sinful," (Rom. vii. 13;) and, as dying *unto* sin was still a strange doctrine to him, he was utterly unwilling to die *by* sin; and therefore strove with all his might to get the mastery over it, that he might live by righteousness. Stung by the commandment, sin would take occasion daily to gnaw at the fair flower of his self-righteousness, making it fade and droop; but daily also

all honour and respect to my poor parents, God bless them! What's the next?" "Thou shalt do no murder." "Thank God, that's not on my conscience. I never slew a man, not even in lawful war. Go on." "Thou shalt not commit adultery." "Of that I have kept clear also, and always been faithful to your poor mother. Proceed." "Thou shalt not steal." "I never took aught did not belong to me. Next." "Thou shalt not bear false witness against thy neigbour." "I never was summoned as witness, nor would I swear falsely against any person. Are there any more?" "Yes, one: Thou shalt not covet." Stop, Jack! there, I must think a little; yes, I cannot say I have never coveted. Pray, look for poor mamma's Bible on the subject." And here Jack found a reference from Exod. xx. to Matt. v., by which the upright farmer was soon led to see that he had broken the whole, and, becoming fully conscious of his exceeding sinfulness, he betook himself to that Christ whom Paul preached, and died a penitent.—Tr.

would he water it anew by self-imposed acts of a legal martyrdom, and thus prolong its artificial existence. And why was he so careful and zealous? whom did he really serve? He indeed imagined that he was serving the God of his fathers, while in fact he was committing sacrilege. (Rom. ii. 22;) because all the while only feeding the pride of that high and noble youth " of the stock of Israel, of the tribe of Benjamin, an Hebrew of the Hebrews; as touching the law, a Pharisee," (Phil. iii. 5.) O Saul! " thou art wearied in the greatness of thy way; yet saidst thou not, There is no hope: thou hast found the life of thine hand; therefore thou wast not grieved,' (Isa. lvii. 10.)

More sharply Paul could not have condemned his Pharisaism, more severely he could not have proved his own infatuated self-deception of this period, than by the words we have chosen for the motto of this chapter, "I was alive without the law once." And herewith he does not mean the life of his childhood, when yet unconscious of the law's "Thou shalt," and "Thou shalt not;" when lust had not yet appeared unto him as sin, and death not been felt by him as the punishment of it. For he adds, "and I died." But if this death had taken place on his first awakening to a consciousness of the law, he could no longer have "found the life of his own hand," and of his Pharisaism there would have been an end. This was not the case; on the contrary, unwilling to the last to concede the "killing letter" a right over him, he continued his utmost efforts to ward off the death-thrusts of the law by trying to turn its flaming testimony against sin into a quenching engine against God's wrath. Thus, though in truth panting under the burden of the law, he fancied himself to be "alive without the law;" while, by his righteousness after the law, he constantly, but fruitlessly, sought to secure this imaginary life against the consuming

B

fire of that very law, the brightness of which no man can bear to behold. Out of the wretchedness of this experience he speaks, when he says, "But even unto this day, when Moses is read, the vail is upon their heart," (2 Cor. iii. 15.) Only from behind this vail, woven thick as scales out of the illusions of man's free-will, can man bear to look upon the law, and take it to be the strength of righteousness, whilst in truth it is the strength of sin, (1 Cor. xv. 56.) Let us rightly understand St Paul's humble confession, " I was alive without the law once." Saul the Pharisee's error certainly was not that he took it over strictly with God's holy commandments. God indeed takes it far more strictly than the strictest Pharisee. On the contrary, his grievous fault was, with a serious face, to play, as it were, at hide-and-seek with the law. But it found him out in every place. Ever nearer and nearer it went to his life; and the issue, alas! of his unhappy marriage with it was one fruit after another brought forth unto death, (Rom. vii. 5.) A legion of lusts, doubts, unbelief, murmurings, or even enmity against the true God of the unflattering and unswerving law; in fine, the entire host of sins lurking in the flesh, revived and issued forth from their hiding-places at law's call; and thus sin by the commandment became exceeding sinful, (Rom vii. 13.) His fancied life "without the law," and the illusion of a righteousness after the Pharisaic phantom of the law, it became daily more difficult for him to maintain; yea it was a life of death nigh unto hell. And yet Saul the Pharisee would rather prolong it by seeking, in hot conflict, to parry the death-stroke of the law, than die under the cry of helpless weakness, "God be merciful to me a sinner!"

That this was pride, Saul would not then acknowledge, being zealous, as he thought, not for his own honour, but for that of the God of Israel; and indignant, not so much against the reproach of human nature, as being too weak to work God's righteousness, but rather the blasphemous thought that the law was unable to effect it. The inability of the former to be "subject to the law of God" (Rom. viii. 7,) he would not own, for the very reason that this admission would imply the other, that "the law was weak through the flesh," (Rom. viii. 3;) which must have shaken his faith in God altogether, for Him he knew not yet, who, by His perfect obedience to the will of God, and His atoning death for sinners, has brought in another righteousness, even that of faith. An adulterer, therefore, in the sense of Rom. vii. 3, Saul would have become, had he escaped from under the yoke of righteousness by the law, ere he knew of another, by faith in Christ Jesus. Thus, then, he was a very different man from those who boast of their freedom from the law without any "obedience to the faith," or, in other words, who make void the law, instead of establishing it through faith, (Rom. iii. 31.) To his experience rather that word of Christ would come home, "If any man will do His will, he shall know of the doctrine, whether it be of God, or whether I speak of myself," (John vii. 17.) This will of God, Saul found expressed in the law, to fulfil which he set to work all the powers of *his* will, in order only to learn that he was a lost and condemned sinner, needing a Saviour such as Christ Jesus. Though, indeed, Paul himself would give us the lie, were we to say that God had manifested His Son to him in reward of his earnestness and sincerity, (Rom ix. 16, xi. 6:) yet—to agree with Paul—we shall be correct in saying, that God's grace followed him in all the ways of his infatuated blindness, till, by the repeated chastisements of the law, as " our schoolmaster to bring us unto Christ," (Gal. iii. 24,) he was so "wearied in the greatness of his way," that it needed but "the heavenly voice," in order to throw himself at once and completely into the arms of his merciful Saviour. He that was to become a Paul, strong by grace of faith, had first to experience in Saul his utter inability to acquire a righteousness by the deeds of the law. The Jews' advantage over the Gentiles in their possessing the Revelation, served to sharpen the accusations of their conscience through the broken law, in order that the true Israel, that is, the Church of Christ—being raised on the wrecks of Judaism—might, through grace, let the doctrine of righteousness by faith in Christ shine resplendent through all lands, to the joy of all true children of Abraham, (cf. Rom. iii. and iv., and Gal. iii.)

Saul, the Pharisee, and Luther, the Austin friar, form a pair. The sophists, at whose feet Luther sat and studied his divinity, were very dexterous in the art of weaving veils, not only for Moses and the prophets, but also for Christ and His apostles, in order to conceal both the splendour of the law and the comforting light of the gospel, and thus to place in advantageous relief the bright shining qualities of the natural man. But for all that, Luther came under anguish of sin by the terrors of the law; the lightning-conductors fabricated by the "idle" scholastics to ward off its strokes did not shield him. As Saul at Jerusalem was intent on gaining merit by the diligent keeping of the Jewish ordinances, or pacifying the accusations of his conscience by legal acts of devotion and self-sacrifice, so Luther, in the monastery at Erfurt. Therefore, after Christ had shined into both their hearts, Luther learnt so thoroughly to understand Paul, that, unawed by the opposition of Romish pharisees and scribes—strutting along against him with proofs, wherewith he himself, as monk, had endeavoured in vain to pacify his alarmed soul—he went on boldly to exalt Christ's blood and righteousness as the only remedy and refuge for sinners. "If there was ever any man," he could say, after the manner of Paul, (Acts xxii. 3, &c.; Phil. iii. 4–6,) "who held in repute the Pope's ordinances, and was zealous for the traditions of our fathers, it was I, who have heartily defended and looked upon them as holy relics, and upon their observance as indeed necessary to salvation; yea, to keep them inviolate I have tormented my body with fasting, watching, prayer, and other exercises, more than all who are now mine enemies and persecutors; for I thought in this wise to satisfy the law, and shield my conscience from the rod of the oppressor. Yet it availed me naught; yea, the further I proceeded in this way the more terrified I grew, so that I had nigh despaired, had not Christ mercifully looked upon me, and enlightened my heart by the light of His Gospel."

And when Paul "testified" to his countrymen "the kingdom of God, persuading them concerning Jesus, both out of the law of Moses and out of the prophets," (Acts xxviii. 23, &c.,) what else did he do but convince his blind brethren that, though living under the law, they were, as he himself had once been, "alive without the law;" that with all their boast of the law, they mistook and denied the power of it? Ever and anon, during his unwearied apostolic labours, would his former life as Pharisee come fresh to his memory. Made himself a true Israelite, who, "through the law," had become "dead to the law," (Gal. ii. 19,) he still, in his "kinsmen according to the flesh," had to re-taste over and over again, to the very dregs, the enmity of false Israelites, who, under the law, lived without the law. But the Church has now, in the apostolic teaching of this former Pharisee, to enjoy the fruit of that seed which fell into such deeply-furrowed soil. The very first sermon St Luke has recorded of him, (at Antioch in Pisidia,) how beautifully clear is its evangelical tone!

"Be it known unto you, therefore, men and brethren, that through this man is preached unto you the forgiveness of sins: and by Him all that believe are justified from all things, from which ye could not be justified by the law of Moses," (Acts xiii. 38, 39;) and in the Romans he sums up the preaching of the faith in this short sentence, "Christ is the end of the law for righteousness to every one that believeth," (Rom. x. 4.)

Gamaliel, Saul's teacher, is celebrated to this day among the Jews as the author of a terrible prayer of theirs against Jesus of Nazareth. Who made Saul to differ? The persecutor of Jesus in His people knew no other cause of his salvation than simply God's mercy in Christ.

> "Saul would not die, but his whole soul was bent
>     To satisfy the law, and thereby live.
> He scorn'd the thought that God's law should be meant
>     To kill, instead of righteousness to give;
> Yea, and the more he had its smart to feel,
> The more he grew beyond his peers in zeal."

## III.

## THE PERSECUTOR.

"I persecuted this way unto the death."—Acts xxii. 4.

"YE have received the law by the disposition of angels, and have not kept it!" exclaimed Stephen before the Council; and they were cut to the heart, gnashing on him with their teeth, (Acts vii. 53, 54.) How deeply the arrow of this word penetrated into Saul's heart, we may gather from the manner in which, about sixteen\* years after, he alludes to the same glorious manifestation of the law upon Sinai, (Gal. iii. 19; cf. also Heb. ii. 2.) Stephen's whole speech was of a nature to stir to the utmost the enmity against Jesus and His followers in the heart of our pharisaic zealot for God, for His law, and His people; for, while ascribing to God's gracious choice and forbearing mercy alone all the glory shining through Israel's history, Stephen, with all the fire of a holy zeal for God, renewed the cutting arraignment of God's servant of old against the rebellious children of Israel, "Understand, therefore, that the Lord thy God giveth thee not this good land to possess it for

---

\* This period is evidently too short. From Gal. i. 17, 18, and ii. 1, more than seventeen years must have elapsed between Acts ix. and xv. And supposing Paul's stay at Antioch (xv. 33) ever so short, and his epistle written after his first visit to Galatia, (xvi. 6,) during his stay at Corinth, (xviii. 11,) a period of very near *twenty years* must lie between Stephen's martyrdom and Paul's Epistle to the Galatians.—TR.

thy righteousness; for thou art a stiff-necked people. Ye have been rebellious against God from the day that I knew you," (Deut. ix. 6, 24; cf. Acts vii. 51.) The very privileges of which the Jews were so proud, (Rom. ix. 4, 5) he arrayed as witnesses against a disobedient and gainsaying people : They are *of Israel*, but not of the faith of Abraham; theirs is the *adoption*, but they deny and betray to the heathen the mystery of it, as did their fathers; theirs is the *glory*, and they profane and desecrate the Temple of God ; the *covenant*, and of its ordinances, circumcision and the *passover*, they make a false trust for their uncircumcised and unbelieving hearts; the *law*, and they have neither kept it, nor known and acknowledged, as its fulfiller, Him of whom Moses testified; the *service of God*, and instead of redeeming mercy, they rejoice in the sacrifices of their own hand; the *promises*, and they believe them not; theirs are the *fathers*, and verily they are the children of those their fathers, who envied Joseph, and sold him into Egypt, " but God was with him;" finally, from them came *Christ*, " who is over all, God blessed for ever;" and Stephen thus accuses them : " Which of the prophets have not your fathers persecuted ? And they have slain them which shewed before of the coming of the Just One; of whom ye have been now the betrayers and murderers."

Saul lived heart and soul in the history of his nation. He now saw the sanctuary of his holy devotion defamed and condemned, and the whole fabric of his pharisaic notions of national glory torn and shattered. Let no one wonder, then, that Stephen's speech went like a sharp saw through his very heart. While accusing the holy Pharisees, one and all, of injustice and the breach of the law, Stephen had called Jesus the " Just One ; " and therewith had struck wounds into Saul's conscience, to bind up which, his tormented soul would labour day and night. To the heart of this youthful zealot, before whose zeal people were already bowing, the conviction would come home with irresistible force: *Either Stephen or I;* there can be no compromise between us; either Stephen has spoken the truth, and then I am lost and undone, or I have been rightly instructed in history and Holy Writ, and then this Jesus of Nazareth must have been a false prophet, and his disciple is guilty of death. A last struggle this decision would inevitably cost him; but so strongly was the notion of pharisaic sanctity engrained in his flesh, that with prayerful imprecations in Jehova's name he would soon be led to reject, as a fiendish temptation, every doubt as to the correctness of the historical authorities represented by the heads of his nation. Thus his rencontre with Stephen would form an important turning point in Saul's life, and serve to hasten to its last climax his inveterate zeal against Jesus of Nazareth and His followers. From this time, then, he was resolved to "persecute this way unto the death." To serve the God of his fathers was a life and death question with him, and the one point at stake was, Who is that God? Is it He who in His Christ upon the cross has held judgment over the sins of the world, "to declare His righteousness," which no flesh, not even that of Israel, can satisfy, but which requires the atoning sacrifice of Christ's blood, in order to save by grace those who believe in Him; or is it He who will send His Christ to defy the lawless heathen, and rescue from their oppression His chosen people, keeping the law in righteousness, and to whom, in reward for their obedience, He will give the world for a possession? Is it He who, upon the instigation of the Jews, has delivered His Christ into the hands of the Gentiles to be scourged and crucified by order of Pontius Pilate, before whom He declared that His kingdom was not of this world, and thereby traced His people's way through it to be likewise one of suffering and death? or is it He who will send His Christ to "judge the world with righteousness and the people with His truth," (Ps. xcvi. 13,) but establish for His own the kingdom of Israel in cloudless glory? Finally, is it He who has sent the Spirit of His Christ—now exalted to His right hand in heaven—into the hearts of His people, that they should serve Him, whose "kingdom is not meat and drink, but righteousness and peace and joy in the Holy Ghost," and that, living in hope of becoming "joint-heirs with Christ," they should reckon the sufferings of this present time as not worthy to be compared with the glory which shall be revealed in them," (Rom. viii. 17, 18); or is it He who will make His Christ appear to His chosen people in visible and palpable glory, and so save all Israel at once by transforming her present state of helpless servitude into one of kingly rule and heavenly felicity, thus fulfilling the prayer of our fathers, "Oh that the salvation of Israel were come out of Zion! When the Lord bringeth back the captivity of His people, Jacob shall rejoice, and Israel shall be glad," (Ps. xiv. 7.) In his zeal for the glory of the law, Saul persecuted Him who bore the curse of the law; in his enthusiasm for the national honour of Israel, he persecuted "the glory of Irael," (Luke ii. 32,) whom Pilate in mockery styled "the King of the Jews;" and in his carnal-minded enmity to a life of faith he persecuted "the Author and Finisher of our faith," whose "kingdom is not of this world."

"But Stephen, being full of the Holy Ghost, looked stedfastly into heaven, and saw the glory of God, and Jesus standing on the right hand of God, and said, Behold I see the heavens opened, and the Son of man standing on the right hand of God:" while to the eyes of the Jews the heavens were closed, whither Jesus had ascended, whose glory they knew not, (1 Cor. ii. 8.) And shutting their enraged ears, they "ran upon him with one accord, and cast him out of the city, and stoned him;" and the witnesses of his supposed blasphemy, whose office it was to cast the first stone, prepared for their "divine service," (John xvi. 2,) by laying down their clothes at a young man's feet, who was the very soul of this zealous deed—even our youthful Saul "the persecutor." *

> " In all stones they throw at Stephen
> Saul's soul rages, more than even
> Theirs whose clothes lie at his feet.
> While to die is sweet to Stephen,
> For he sees in open heaven
> Jesus whom his soul shall meet."
> ADAM DE ST VICTOR.

"Saul was consenting unto his death," writes St Luke (Acts viii. 1,) and Paul, upon his being won by Christ, thus expresses to the Lord Himself the feeling at his once unhappy participation in this scene, "And when the blood of thy martyr Stephen was shed, I also was standing by, and consenting unto his death, and kept the raiment of them that slew him," (Acts xxii. 20.) Were some Jews, if not most, short-sighted enough to imagine Stephen as possessed of a different spirit from that of the rest of Christ's disciples, Saul, with his penetrating eye, knew better than to think that the grave of this one would close over the name of the Nazarene, unless every one of "this way" could be destroyed with him; and therefore he owns long after, before King Agrippa, "I verily thought with myself that I ought to do many things contrary to the name of Jesus of Naza-

* The celebrated Spanish painter Vicente Joannes has represented Saul as walking at the martyr's side lost in profound meditation, in striking contrast with the wild rabble. Fervent devotion is painted on his face, and upon his brow falls apparently from far off a ray of light that beams from Stephen's face (Acts vi. 15;) but which, with as much difficulty as determination, he evidently forces himself to ward off.

reth," (Acts xxvi. 9,) and the "ravening wolf" of the tribe of Benjamin (Gen. xlix. 27,) deemed it a "profiting in the Jews' religion" when he "persecuted the church of God and wasted it," (Gal. i. 13, 14.) And such was the influence which Saul—a man already even in his youth—exercised over the minds of the people, who hitherto—from the powerful, heavenly demonstrations in their behalf—had evidently regarded the Apostles and their work with reverential awe, if not with favour, (Acts ii. 47, iii. 9-11, iv. 21, v. 13, 26,) that from Stephen's martyrdom he carried them away to a general persecution, he himself their leader, " making havoc of the Church, entered into every house, and haling men and women, committed them to prison, and when they were put to death, he gave his voice against them;" yea and " oft in every synagogue" he punished and " compelled them to blaspheme," thus becoming a murderer of their souls also. Nor did it satisfy his blind zeal for the honour of God and His law to persecute and destroy " this way" in Jerusalem only, but " being exceedingly mad against them," he applied for warrants to the chief priests—to whose Saducean lukewarmness in the cause, the fiery Saul might be now becoming rather irksome at Jerusalem—and went with them, destroying the churches where he came, "even unto strange cities," as far as Damascus, whence from the "scattered" flock of Christ rays of light were already spreading abroad into heathen countries, (Acts viii. 3, 4, ix. 1, 2, xxii. 4, 5, xxvi. 9-11.)

Not only in his defences made at Jerusalem, first before the people, (from the stairs of the chief captain's castle, Acts xxi. 37, 40,) and next before Festus and King Agrippa, does the Apostle speak of his former benighted life, into which the light of grace fell from heaven, but also in his epistles he repeatedly calls to mind the remembrance of his shame, which he had once accounted honour. However much he had learnt to detest it now—having become dead unto sin—yet the memory of his heinous guilt and disgrace would ever revive, to serve him as a continual cause for deèp humiliation; and *divine grace* would indeed shine all the brighter upon the dark background of *nature's disgrace*, to the eternal praise of God's mercy in Christ. Where he most extols his office, and confesses what Christ has wrought through him, he also bows lowest under an overwhelming sense of the grace shewn unto him, and writes, " I am the least of the apostles, that am not meet to be called an apostle, because I persecuted the church of God," (1 Cor. xv. 9 ; cf. Eph. iii. 8.) An " untimely birth " he calls himself, not only " as one born out of due time," (1 Cor. xv. 8,) but also as being, by the skilful hand of Jesus, the heavenly physician, withdrawn (" separated," if not torn) from the bosom of false Judaism. The Galatians—who, through some Judaisers that troubled them, were led to look upon the Apostle's gospel of Christian liberty as human—he reminds of his " conversation in time past in the Jewish religion," from which neither himself nor any man, but solely the grace of God, " by the revelation of Jesus Christ," had delivered him, (Gal. i. 11, &c.) Above all, to Timothy, his " own son in the faith," the Apostle pours out his whole heart. Being deeply solicitous that he should hold fast the form of sound words, " which he had heard of him, " in faith and love which is in Christ Jesus," he draws for Timothy, in his own inimitable manner, the picture of that man from whom he had learnt Christ, and to whose " trust the glorious Gospel of the blessed God had been committed." " I thank Christ Jesus our Lord," he writes, " who hath enabled me, for that he counted me faithful, putting me into the ministry; who was before a blasphemer, and a persecutor, and injurious; but I obtained mercy, because I did it ignorantly in unbelief. And the grace of our Lord was exceeding abundant, with faith and love which is in Christ Jesus. This is a faithful saying, and worthy of all acceptation, that Christ Jesus came into the world to save sinners, of whom I am chief. Howbeit for this cause I obtained mercy, that in me first Jesus Christ might shew forth all long-suffering for a pattern to them which should hereafter believe on him to life everlasting," (1 Tim. i. 12–16.)

Stephen's dying prayer, "Lord, lay not this sin to their charge," could be answered for Saul the persecutor, because he was one of those for whom Christ prayed upon the cross, "Father, forgive them, for they know not what they do." St Paul was far from entertaining the ungodly notion that, because, as persecutor, he had, to the best of his conscience, acted in accordance with his conviction, therefore his "zeal to God," though "not according to knowledge," (Rom. x. 2,) had availed aught before Him in procuring his favour and acceptance. No, rather his conscience, when "purified by faith," accused him of damnable sin, from which Christ, of His own mere grace, had saved him. "But I obtained mercy," he says, "because, being ignorant, I did it in unbelief." To this we firmly hold, while seeing in the persecutor's zeal the spirit of the iron-hearted Jew and warlike Benjamite, which, sanctified by grace, made him the champion he became in the cause of Christ. Nearer, indeed, to the kingdom of God, was Saul the persecutor, than is that lukewarm generation of worldlings, who, either from drowsy indifference, or absorption in material interests, will never be at the pains of troubling the Church of Christ. In the burning zeal and thorough earnestness wherewith Saul consumed himself, as he "was breathing out threatenings and slaughter against the disciples of the Lord," (Acts ix. 1;) in the manly firmness wherewith he concentrated all upon this one thing, the extirpation of the followers of the Cross, as the arch-enemies to his arch-Judaism, there were mightily though mistakenly (" in unbelief ") at work those vigorous natural powers he bore along from his mother's womb, which, turned by grace into their right direction, (faith in Christ,) made him the unswerving soldier and herald of the Cross. Luther, in his naïve manner, says, " Now, when Saul took the matter so to heart, the Lord Jesus had His thoughts about it, and said to Himself, ' Wait a little, that man will turn out well; for what he does, he does in right earnest. The fervour he now shews in a bad cause, I will still increase by my Spirit, and apply to a good cause. He shall preach of me among the Gentiles, which shall stir up the Jews, as they deserve, to become quite mad and foolish, as he himself has hitherto been.' Just as our Lord God uses me now against the Pope and his band, for whom formerly I would have gone through the fire, and now none fights more bitterly against them."

Not forgetting what once he was, Paul enters, with as much meekness as firmness, upon his new path full of thorns, where step by step, and on all sides, he is met by the same pharisaic spirit of persecution he himself had heretofore displayed. View him at Jerusalem under the murderous blows of his blind countrymen, whose souls he is seeking to win in tenderest and devoted love. Hear him as, standing before an enraged multitude, (Acts xxi. 35, &c.,) he wins their silence by his meek address, (Acts xxii. 1, &c.), " Men, brethren, and fathers," and then continues, " I was zealous towards God, as ye all are this day, and I persecuted this way unto the death." This meekness Paul learnt in the school of Christ's Spirit, who reminded him of his own past life, of abounding sin, and of far more abounding grace.

> Saul's zeal grew rage, and this to slaughter led;
> Nor would aught give content to his fierce soul

But persecution to the very death,
Till of that way he had destroy'd the whole.
And this dread zeal was with religion pair'd:
For thus he thought to serve his people's God.
" In ignorance," as after he declared,
" And unbelief," he trod this fearful road.
But Satan should not triumph over Saul;
For we shall witness next his heavenly call.

## IV.

## THE WON OF THE LORD JESUS.

*" Where sin abounded, grace did much more abound."*—ROM. v. 20.

AMBROSE calls the conversion of Paul the most glorious deed of Christ the King—next to the outpouring of the Holy Spirit. Glorious, indeed, in its fruit—the gathering of the Gentiles into the fold of Christ, through the gospel of His grace preached by this child of grace; and glorious also in the sovereign power of Divine grace which wrought it, and became the inexhaustible theme of praise in the mouth of this won one of the Lord Jesus.

How great Paul's conversion and call was in the eyes of St Luke, is clear from his thrice recounting its history with evident delight: once in the thread of his own narrative, where the patient sun, that has sent forth his first rays of the evangelical day over the Jewish nation, begins already to draw toward evening for that nation; and twice in the great Apostle's defence of the Gospel at Jerusalem, where night is already fast closing in upon them, (Acts ix., xxii., xxvi.) Let us take a connected review of this threefold account.

It was not, we may be sure, without heartfelt thanks to God for thus permitting him to do Him service, (John xvi. 2,) that Saul, furnished with commissions from the high priest, entered upon the honourable mission of the Jewish holy inquisition—to go abroad after Christ's disciples, haling men and women, and bringing them bound unto Jerulem. But, lo! as he sped on his way to Damascus, and drew nigh to the city, suddenly, about noon, there shined round about him a light from heaven, above the brightness of the sun. It was even the Lord Jesus Christ, the same whom Stephen saw in the opened heavens, standing on God's right hand, who now appeared to Saul, (1 Cor. ix. 1, xv. 8,) dazzling his eyes with the glorious light of His countenance. They also that were with him saw indeed the light, before which the noontide sun grew pale, but they saw no man; they heard the sound of a voice, "but they heard not," St Paul says, "the voice of Him that spake to me." "And when we were all fallen to the ground," he continues, "I heard a voice speaking unto me, and saying in the Hebrew tongue, Saul, Saul, why persecutest thou me?" So, then, He whom Saul persecutes is throned in heaven; and Stephen spoke the truth; Saul is the man of death! and yet he lives; the glare of His heavenly majesty hath darted upon, but not slain him. "Why persecutest thou me?" In this appeal to Saul's heart, of Him who is glorious and terrible, is blended the voice of mercy. "What have I done unto thee, O my people? and wherein have I wearied thee? testify against me," (Micah vi. 3.) Crushed by the overwhelming sense of his extreme guiltiness, Saul lay prostrate in the dust, yet upheld and drawn, at the same time, by the arms of that long-suffering mercy, which hereafter he knows so well to exhibit to his unhappy brethren according to the flesh, (Rom. x. 21.) The mystery of that grace which, without coercing, draws with irresistible force—which wins and conquers by no other weapons than those of tender intreaty and imploring love—now began to dawn upon Saul's mind, as he ventured to put the question, "Who art thou, Lord?" That He who from heaven called him by name, and whose glory he saw, was the Lord, the living God, he was sure enough, and needed no further proof; but that it was He whom he had been persecuting, this thought seized him like a stroke of lightning, falling on him unawares, and penetrating to his very inmost soul. *Him* whose name he has cursed, and whom he has persecuted as a blasphemer, he now beholds in heavenly glory, yea, and hears Him pronounce His own name—"I am *Jesus* whom thou persecutest,"—that name above every name, (Phil. ii. 10,) by which He is worshipped and adored, both in heaven and earth, as the Lord and Saviour of His believing people, "who, crucified through weakness, liveth by the power of God," (2 Cor. xiii. 4,) and out of His own mouth ("Why persecutest thou *me?*") he now learns that "great mystery" of the oneness of "Christ and the Church," (Eph. v. 32;) He the head, she the body, and believers on earth "members in particular of the body of Christ," (1 Cor. xii. 27)—a favourite subject henceforth of the Apostle's teaching and devout adoration. How may the exalted Saviour have looked upon this fruit "of the travail of His soul;" the youth of His choice, whom He had "loved with an everlasting love," and was now drawing to Himself "with the cords of love!" And Stephen, was he permitted, too, to look down upon this "strong one" whom Jesus took for His "spoil" that day? More than the angels of God must he have rejoiced at this first-fruit of his martyrdom. But Satan must have beheld with rage and gnashing of teeth this victory of the Lord Jesus; nor would he stand an idle beholder of the scene, but summon to his aid the art of hell, for in this one prey he would lose a thousand, yea, countless legions in the lapse of time. And Jesus, on His part, will not triumph over him by some enchantment, as it were, of Saul, stronger than Satan's; but says to His won one, "It is hard for thee to kick against the pricks."

Hard, yet not impossible. This Saul has clearly learnt, for he says, "I was *not disobedient* to the heavenly voice;" which he might have been, had he not at once "brought into captivity every thought to the obedience of Christ," (2 Cor. x. 5,) and resisted the serpent's subtle beguilement to "corrupt his mind from the simplicity in Christ," (2 Cor. xi. 3.) Against the pricks of Divine wrath Saul had hitherto kicked. Like as the ox kicks against the staff of the driver, so Saul had been kicking against the deadly pricks of the law, which entered but the more deeply into his flesh the more he endeavoured to satisfy Divine justice by a self-acquired unblamable righteousness. But now the grace of the Lord Jesus would make it too hard for him any longer to continue this suicidal labour. The pricks of the avenger are broken in the flesh of Christ crucified, who in His own body upon the cross has "slain the enmity thereby," (Eph. ii. 16.) So long as Saul persecuted Jesus he wanted to redeem his own soul, which costs too much, "so that he must let that alone for ever," (Ps. xlix. 8, Prayer Book transl.) But now it came to a happy crisis, a solution worth the whole world, (Matt. xvi. 26.) In the death of Christ there now appeared to him the end of the law warring against the sinner, and in His resurrection the entering in of that righteousness which both satisfies God and gives peace to the sinner that believeth in Christ, (Rom. iii. 26, iv. 25, v. 1; Eph. ii. 17.) But ere *Paul* could attain to the blessed experience of being "dead with Christ, and buried with Him in baptism," *Saul* had first to taste that bitter dying described in Rom. vii. 9-11, "And I died." Here, before the gates of Damascus—"smitten to the ground by the law," as Luther says—he felt its sharp-pointed arrow fasten deep into his heart; he was accursed, and deserved to hang on that tree where Jesus his Saviour hung for him. Will he still kick against the pricks, now

that he has beheld the law which "worketh wrath" in the light of overpowering grace? No, it has become too hard for him. Trembling and astonished, but withal still bent upon penitential obedience, he cries out, "Lord, what wilt thou have me to do?" In this hour of anguish, "as the terrors of God flashed through his soul," it would surely have been the greatest relief to him, had the Lord exacted of him a penitence and satisfaction ever so bitter and severe. In none of these, however, but solely in the all-availing sacrifice and satisfaction made by Jesus Christ once for all upon the cross, could he find rest; and he has found it. It was only by opening his sad heart to this same Jesus, that he felt his own sins also were atoned for and cancelled. With encouraging gentleness, the Lord then bids him "rise and stand upon his feet;" but forthwith, to test his obedience, He adds: "And go into the city, and it shall be told thee what thou must do." In thus commissioning him to apply for instruction to the believers at Damascus, those very people he had hitherto persecuted, the Lord greatly honoured His Church, and vindicated to her the high office and blessed privilege of dispensing to sinners the means of His grace. In the Church only would He be found of him with absolution to eternal peace.\*
And with such docility did Saul enter into this Divine order of grace, and so completely does Paul afterwards identify Christ and the Church, that in his speech before Agrippa he passes the mediating Ananias clean by, and affirms to have heard of Jesus what Ananias told him in His name.†

On rising from the ground, Saul perceived that he was

---

\* Once for all, I here repeat—what impliedly I have averred in my prefatory remark on the subject—that I do not concur in the author's *High Church views*.—TR.

† Great nicety linked with ingenuity.—TR.

blind. Hitherto he had said, "I see," (John ix. 41;) now he finds his spiritual blindness portrayed upon his bodily eyes, which are blinded by the glory of the heavenly vision. In this pitiable plight, yet resigned to Jesus's custody, he is led by the hands of his astounded companions, and brought into Damascus. The wolf is turned into a lamb. "And he was three days without sight, and neither did eat nor drink,"—seeking and finding the more food for his hungry soul in the Word of God and the teaching of His Church; yea, while his bodily eyes failed him, his inner eyes would open to the voice of the prophets, giving him answer to the Lord's question : "Saul, Saul, why persecutest thou me?" and in the penitential psalms he would find the fittest utterance for his unutterable woe. "We know that the law is spiritual; but I am carnal, sold under sin," (Rom. vii. 14.) This knowledge of a contrite sinner was now beaming upon him in the light of that transcendent fact—that He who had hung upon the accursed tree was now exalted to heavenly glory and Divine majesty. Now he had torn from his bleeding heart "what things were gain" to him, (Phil. iii. 7;) and, dying, waited for *His* help, who by His word, "I am Jesus!" had already breathed on him the Spirit of life. Saul spent three days of anguish in the deep ere he ascended to the height. "Behold, he prayeth," said the Lord, by way of encouragement to Ananias, who still dreaded the man of slaughter. "Behold, he prayeth;" a precious word, as it proves to us that the humble prayer of a contrite sinner goes direct to the heart of Jesus in heaven, who enlists for the penitent the sympathy of His believing children on earth, yea, and the service of His swift-flying angels in heaven, (Dan. ix. 20–23.) The Lord answering Saul's prayer through the mouth of a "disciple" and fellow-sinner does not contradict Gal. i. 11, 12, where Paul declares that the Gospel he preached he had neither received of man, nor been taught it, but by the revelation of Jesus Christ. For the substance of his preaching to others—viz., the Gospel of the grace of our Lord Jesus Christ—was indeed communicated to him by the revelation of that same Jesus who appeared unto him from heaven; but of his own pardon and acceptance by Him through the same grace he was to receive the comforting assurance in no other way than every other sinner accepted by Christ—viz., through the ordinary means of grace—the Word and Sacrament. Also that he might receive again his sight and be filled with the Holy Ghost was Ananias sent to him from God. Yea, so highly did the Lord honour His poor persecuted church at Damascus, that He announced to Ananias, when yet they were trembling at Saul's approach, the triumph of His grace over this persecutor of Himself in His people; and upon Ananias still hesitating, alleging in child-like simplicity the terror-stirring accounts they had heard of "this man," the Lord bids him "Go thy way; for he is a chosen vessel unto me, to bear my name before the Gentiles and kings and the children of Israel: For I will shew him how great things he must suffer for my name's sake." Thus the Lord not only laid the new convert in the arms of the Church, but made over to her the "chosen vessel" also.

To extol Israel's glory in the sight of the heathen had been Saul's inmost desire; and because he had taken the followers of Jesus to be the enemies to Israel's glory, therefore he had persecuted them. But, won himself of the Lord Jesus, out of the lost children of Israel, he was now to bear His name, as the banner of salvation, before the Gentiles and their kings; and, by gathering them into "the Israel of God," he was to provoke fallen Israel to rise again, (Rom. xi. 11, &c.) That Christ's kingdom should be one of suffering and death had been his great offence, because he could not reconcile the Cross with the carnal thoughts of his Jewish prejudices. But now he goes to "confirm the souls of the disciples, exhorting them, that we must through much tribulation enter into the kingdom of God," (Acts xiv. 22;) yea, and as their ministering servant in Christ, himself goes to bear in his own flesh, and that with joy, of "the afflictions of Christ," which the church militant has to "fill up"—that measure of suffering meet for so great an apostle, (Col. i. 24.)

Ere Ananias entered the house of Judas in the street called "Straight" at Damascus, and inquired for one called Saul of Tarsus, the Lord had already shewn to praying Saul in a vision this very man coming in and putting his hand on him. Thus his humbly-yielding soul was fully prepared for the visit, and longed for this messenger of his Saviour. "Brother Saul," said Ananias, on entering and laying his hands on him, "the Lord, even Jesus that appeared unto thee in the way as thou camest, hath sent me" (the good Shepherd hath found His sheep on the way, beside a yawning precipice) "that thou mightest receive thy sight, and be filled with the Holy Ghost;" with the recovery of thy bodily sight to receive enlightened eyes of the mind, that thou mayest know the blessed hope of the won and called of Jesus Christ. Then Saul, "looking up upon him," heard this true Israelite further declare unto him, "The God of our fathers hath chosen thee" with an everlasting calling in Christ, "that thou shouldest know His will" of salvation, carried into effect from Abraham's call down to the raising up of the horn of salvation in the house of his servant David, (Acts xiii. 16, &c.;) and see that "Just One," who by His knowledge shall justify many, for He shall bear their iniquity, (Isa. liii. 11;) and shouldest hear the voice of His mouth for a testimony that Jesus Christ is declared to be the Son of God with power, (Rom. i. 4.) "For thou shalt be His witness unto all men of what thou hast seen and heard, and of those things in the which He will appear unto thee."

Paul's apostolic witness is born out of Saul's inner history; it is altogether that of his personal experience of the grace of God in Christ Jesus his Lord. Bright, indeed, over his apostolical career do the stars shine whereby the Lord so wonderfully guided the footsteps of His chosen servant from Jerusalem even unto Rome, (Acts xxii. 17; Gal. ii. 2; Acts xvi. 9, xviii. 9, 10, xxiii. 11, xxvii. 23, 24;) but brightest of all shines that "star out of Jacob," which rose to him on his way to Damascus, illuminating the path of his life throughout the marvellous sphere of his labour of love, chastening his joys, and supporting him under all afflictions; for this star had shined into his very heart, (2 Cor. iv. 6; Gal. i. 16.) With the testimony of the Lord Jesus, who had won him, and was "revealed in him," Paul went forth—being delivered from the People, who in him thrust from them their last saving-angel, and from all dangers among the Gentiles, unto whom the Lord now sent him—"to open their eyes, and to turn them from darkness unto light, and from the power of Satan unto God, that they might receive forgiveness of sins, and inheritance among them which are sanctified by faith that is in Christ Jesus," (Acts xxvi. 18.) To this "inheritance" Saul himself was now being admitted. "And now, why tarriest thou?" said Ananias, (who saw him still kneel in rapt amazement before the opened door of heavenly grace.) "Arise, and be baptized, and wash away thy sins, calling on the name of the Lord." "And immediately," Luke writes, "there fell from his eyes as it had been scales; and he received sight forthwith, and arose and was baptized." With new eyes he now beheld the aged messenger of the Lord Jesus. So he had never before looked upon any of His disciples. Stephen's angel-face would again rise up before his soul, and make him exclaim, " O, that I had known Thee sooner, fairest of the sons of men!" Now was Saul planted in the likeness of Christ's death, being " buried with Him by baptism; that, like as Christ was raised up from the dead by the glory of the Father, even so he also should walk in newness of life," (Rom. vi. 4;) and now, having received the spirit of adoption, he could with a reconciled conscience cry, " Abba, Father." There he stood now, the won of the Lord Jesus, clad in the garments of His salvation, and covered with the robe of righteousness, (Isa. lxi. 10.) " And when he had received meat, he was strengthened." With what feelings may Saul have sat down and partaken of this his first meal with Christ's disciples! And if at the close of it they ate the passover of the New Testament, his heart would indeed be drawn to the True Passover—Christ slain for sinners,—and his overflowing adoration might find utterance in words like these :—

> " Hasten now, my soul, to meet Him,
> And with loving reverence greet Him,
> Who with words of life immortal
> Now is knocking at thy portal;
> Haste to make for Him a way,
> Cast thee at His feet and say:
> Since, O Lord, Thou com'st to me,
> I will never turn from Thee!"

There fell as it had been scales from Saul's eyes immediately as he received his sight. The "veil" was taken away as soon as his soul turned to the Lord, (2 Cor. iii. 16.) Now he understood Stephen's speech. God's plan of Israel's and the world's redemption, as traced by this faithful witness through the history of the Old Testament, now stood in heavenly brightness before his unveiled eyes, all illuminated by that one light—Christ crucified and risen again.

At the head of this picture of Paul's conversion we have placed Rom. v. 20, "Where sin abounded, grace did much more abound;" and the way in which he was won to Christ has shewn us that the mystery of Christ, (Eph. iii. 3, &c.,) which shines so bright through all his apostolical preaching, was intrusted to him as the mystery of his self-experienced grace in the forgiveness of his sins. His person and his work are in harmonious oneness, illuminated both by the same bright splendour of his heavenly calling. Abounding sin and superabounding grace,—these two poles of the Gospel of Christ, about which faith moves,—as they form the main traits of his own Christian character, so they constitute the main points of his apostolical teaching. We shall take occasion to speak of this in another chapter (Paul "the man of faith.") In the next we have to accompany "the labourer of the Lord" into the harvest of the Gentiles, and the last gathering in of the remnant among Israel.

> "To Jesus' love a stranger yet,
>   Saul sped along the road,
> Intent to slay where'er he met
>   Christ's harmless flock abroad;
> When, lo! from heav'n he heard a call,
>   'Twas Jesus' voice, which said,
> Why persecutest thou me, Saul?
>   But rise; for I have made
> A chosen vessel thee, to bear
>   My name before the world;
> And I will shew thee how to share
>   The cross thou shalt unfold."

## V.

### THE LABOURER.

*" I laboured more abundantly than they all."*—1 COR. xv. 10.

WE are not writing the history of Paul's life; yet we must follow him on the way of his apostolical labour, in order to collect the traits of that picture which the Holy Ghost has presented to us in this man of God. "By the grace of God I am what I am," he says, in the same place, where he boldly speaks, "I laboured more abundantly than they all." In his apostolical labour his Christian character is reflected; and in this view let us consider the work he accomplished.

To be found "in labours" the Apostle reckons among those things in which the ministers of God approve themselves, (2 Cor. vi. 4, 5;) and a diligent labourer indeed he was, "not slothful in business, fervent in spirit, serving the Lord," (Rom. xii. 11;) yea, life itself he was ever ready to sacrifice, and that joyfully, in the service of his Heavenly Master, (Phil. ii. 17;) nor was there anything he was more afraid of than "living unto himself," and thus robbing God of His own property—both body and soul belonging unto Him, (Rom. xiv. 7, 8; 1 Cor. vi. 19, 20; 2 Cor. v. 15.) And it was Christ's constraining love, (2 Cor. v. 14,) this grand motive to all his actions, which in the face of "bonds and afflictions" made him declare to the elders of the Ephesian church, "None of these things move me, neither count I my life dear unto myself, so that I might finish my course with joy, and the ministry which I have received of the Lord Jesus, to testify the Gospel of the grace of God," (Acts xx. 24.)

Yet "day rises none the sooner because we rise before dawn." This Paul learned in the school of the Holy Ghost. "In quietness and confidence shall be your strength," (Isa. xxx. 15.) As the silent brook, which hides itself in a glen, is only gathering strength to pour forth more vigorously at large and swell to a mighty stream—so ran the course of our great Apostle's life.. While resting certain days with the disciples at Damascus, he could not indeed refrain from testifying at once what he had heard and seen to the Jews in that city. Impelled by the ardour of his first love, and the clear conviction of his new heart, he straightway proved Christ in their synagogues, that He is the Son of God, (Acts ix. 20.) "Immediately," he says, (Gal. i. 16, 17,) "I conferred not with flesh and blood, neither went I up to Jerusalem to them which were apostles before me," as if they had been more credible witnesses than Ananias, or as if my heavenly call needed their ratification. Still less did he think it his duty to the chief priests whose commission he had held, or to Gamaliel, his former teacher, that he should hear and weigh his and their arguments. But, great as was his ardour, his testimony had not the effect which—" coming fresh from the forge," as Luther says—he expected. For though he "confounded the Jews," by proving that Jesus is the Christ, they were no less offended at his new doctrine than amazed at his sudden change. Then would come home to his heart what Stephen had said of Moses: "For he supposed his brethren would have understood him, how that God by his hand would deliver them, but they understood not," (Acts vii. 25.) Paul, like Moses, was first to serve his apprenticeship in the wilderness. For a three years' stillness the heavenly Master led His disciple into the deserts of Arabia, (Gal. i. 17,) whither he was followed by no Philip to interpret to him God's Word; but the Lord Jesus Himself was his teacher, as he studied the Scriptures and pondered over the kingdom of God; and the glory in which he had beheld Him who was slain for sinners shed its heavenly light over his meditations, illuminating the pages of the prophets, and opening to his spiritual view the progress of Christ's Church and kingdom on earth. If the "visions and revelations of the Lord," (2 Cor. xii. 1,) which he kept above fourteen years to himself, (ib., ver. 2,) fell within the period of these three years, then were not only the three years' companionship of the disciples, but also the forty days that the Lord shewed Himself alive unto them, amply compensated to him by his being "caught up into paradise, and hearing unspeakable words," (ib., ver. 4.) To make all flesh keep silence before Him, God has raised up and fitted for their high calling the greatest of His servants in retirement away from the world,—Moses in Midian, Elijah at the brook Cherith, Paul in Arabia. Nor, when he returned from this lengthened seclusion, had the moment arrived yet for Paul to enter upon his apostolical labour. Chosen and called as he was of Christ, yet would he not proclaim himself, but waited in patient modesty till, after proving before the first heathen congregation his heaven-wrought fitness for the work, the Holy Ghost, by the mouth of the Church, had confirmed the heavenly call of his Master, (Acts xiii. 2;) for he would have no man think of him above that which he saw him to be, or heard of him, (2 Cor. xii. 6.) He loathed all "commending of himself," well knowing that only he is approved "whom the Lord commendeth," (2 Cor. x. 18.) From Arabia he returned again unto Damascus, (Gal. i. 17,) where "the

Jews took counsel to kill him;" and, assisted by the Arabian governor's garrison, "watched the gates day and night," desirous to apprehend him. "But their lying in wait being known of Saul," this "man in Christ," "caught up to the third heaven," even "into paradise," was yet so sober, and so well prepared for the suffering state of Christ's Church on earth, that he allowed the disciples to take him by night, and let him down by the wall in a basket, in order to escape the hands of his pursuers, (Acts ix. 23-25; 2 Cor. xi. 32, 33.) It is for the seeming weakness of this basket-flight, that, at the close of that long register of his sufferings detailed in the last-named chapter, (2 Cor. xi.,) the Apostle adduces this circumstance as a proof that "if he must needs glory, he will glory of the things which concern his infirmity." Now he went up to Jerusalem, which he had not seen again since his conversion. As a persecutor he had left it, as a fugitive he re-entered it. How might he feel as he set his feet within the gates of that beloved city! Yet differently from what his love expected was he received by the Christian congregation. There was no Ananias prepared by a heavenly vision to meet him, and welcome his arrival; yea, rather, as "he assayed to join himself to the disciples, they were all afraid of him, and believed not that he was a disciple. But Barnabas took him, and brought him to the apostles, and declared unto them how he had seen the Lord in the way, and that He had spoken to him," (Acts ix. 26, 27.) When a Pharisee, Saul had been distinguished as a man of consequence among the people; now Paul, when won by Jesus, bore it meekly to have his character shielded by the testimony of Barnabas. With Peter indeed he abode fifteen days, but others of the apostles saw he none, save James the Lord's brother, (Gal. i. 18, 19;) nor was it till "fourteen years after," when he went up to Jerusalem "by revelation," (Gal. ii. 1, 2,) that he was formally recognised as an apostle, and, together with Barnabas, "received the right hands of fellowship," (ib., ver. 9;) "that we should go," he there adds, "unto the heathen, and they unto the circumcision." Thus his heavenly commission was ratified on earth. But what it cost him to give up his favourite wish—to become the herald of salvation to his own brethren after the flesh—may be judged from the circumstance that the Lord again appeared unto him especially for this purpose, in the Temple of Jerusalem, saying unto him, "Make haste, and get thee quickly out of Jerusalem; for they will not receive thy testimony concerning me;" and, upon Paul's reference to his former conduct, as a well-meant apology for their rejection of his testimony, the Lord still more categorically repeated His charge: "Depart, for I will send thee far hence unto the Gentiles," (Acts xxii. 17-21.)

In Tarsus, his native city, Saul was still waiting his Master's pleasure, as to whither He would have him go, till Barnabas sought for him there, and finding him, brought him to Antioch, (Acts xi. 25, 26.) Thus he did not take his apostleship as a robbery. At Antioch they laboured "a whole year" in the church that had been gathered there by "men of Cyprus and Cyrene," whom "the persecution that arose about Stephen" had scattered thither, and abroad into other heathen lands, (Acts xi.) Here, under the deepest sense of God's goodness and severity to bring salvation unto the Gentiles through the fall of the Jews, (Rom. xi. 11,) the Apostle's call to labour among the former virtually began. But immediately also an occasion offered for his helping hand unto those of the circumcision. A "great dearth" happening "in the days of Claudius Cæsar," the disciples of Antioch sent relief unto the brethren which dwelt in Judea by the hands of Barnabas and

Saul, (ib.,) in proof of the close communion existing between the two churches, and to provoke to jealousy the unbelieving Jews. The church at Jerusalem, indeed, was scattered abroad more and more. Upon James's martyrdom and Peter's miraculous escape from prison, (Acts xii.,) the latter also " departed, and went into another place," (ib. ver. 17.)

Now, when Barnabas and Saul were deputed by the church at Antioch, under direction of the Holy Ghost, to the ministry of the Gospel among the Gentiles, (Acts xiii. 1-3,) their course was guided partly by Barnabas's attractions to his native country, Cyprus, (ib. ver. 4,) but chiefly by Paul's apostolic maxim, to preach the Gospel where Christ had not been named, lest he should build upon another man's foundation, (Rom. xv. 20; 2 Cor. x. 16.) At Salamis, the capital of Cyprus, we see the true Israelite meet in combat with false Judaism about the Roman deputy's soul; and here, with Elymas the sorcerer, Saul maintained his first open contest with "the rulers of the darkness of this world," (Eph. vi. 12.) In many incidents of his life the Apostle seems sensible of personal powers of darkness withstanding his labour of light and love, were it only a casual hindrance in the way of paying a ministerial visit, (1 Thess. ii. 18.) While he knows Christ, and is known of Him, he is not ignorant of Satan's devices, (2 Cor. ii. 11.) Having rescued the deputy's soul out of the net of Elymas,—that "sorcerer" and "child of the devil,"—St Luke, as if in honour of this first prize won by him for Christ in the person of Sergius Paulus, changes Saul's name into that of Paul, (Acts xiii. 9,) and gives him precedence henceforth over Barnabas. It is not unlikely, though, that already, on occasion of his baptism, the Apostle, prompted by Christian humility, may have desired this change in his name; for Paul means "little," while Saul means "asked," "desired." His parents, perhaps, had long prayed for him; and, lo! like the ill-asked king of old, their son also became a persecutor of God's beloved. But now, as Paul the little, or "less than the least," he would lay all Saul's greatness and gain at the King of Israel's feet, and say with David, "Thou hast given me the defence of thy salvation; thy right hand also shall hold me up, and thy loving correction shall make me great," (Ps. xviii. 35.)

Reaching next to Antioch in Pisidia, they "went into the synagogue on the Sabbath-day, and sat down." From first to last the Apostle of the Gentiles yields to the Jews in their dispersion the place he assigns them in that cardinal passage, "To the Jew first," (Rom. i. 16.) The sermon he now preaches in their synagogue is a striking evidence of the deep impression Stephen's speech had made on his mind, for his own is almost the exact counterpart of it, (Acts xiii. 16–41.) He lit up the lamp of Israel by tracing the prophetic word to its accomplishment in Christ, whose inestimable value to their souls he summed up in ver. 38, 39. The effect was considerable, (ver. 42, 43.) But, lo! on the very next Sabbath the Jews were filled with envy against the Gentiles, (ver. 45.) Then, upon their "contradicting and blaspheming," "Paul and Barnabas waxed bold, and said, It was necessary that the word of God should first have been spoken to you: but seeing ye put it from you, and judge yourselves unworthy of everlasting life, lo, we turn to the Gentiles: for so hath the Lord commanded us, saying, I have set thee to be a light of the Gentiles, that thou shouldest be for salvation unto the ends of the earth," (ib. ver. 46, 47; Isa. xlix. 6.) Thus early had the Apostle to experience that his labour of joy among the Gentiles—for "they glorified the word of the Lord," which was published throughout all the region—was to him likewise a labour of sorrow; inasmuch as the Lord accomplished His judgment upon the "despisers," (ver. 41,) declared by His prophets, (Isa. xxix. 14; Hab. i. 5,) through the preaching of Paul, who trod in their footsteps. And if ever his hope had been sanguine enough to expect that whole cities and provinces would, upon his preaching of Christ, turn to the Lord, his experience in Pisidia already would have taught him otherwise. Yet "as many," St Luke writes, (ver. 48,) "as were ordained to eternal life believed." Only those who by grace were led to believe in Christ accepted the call of God's everlasting purpose of love in Him, and their names were written in the book of life; while the disobedient and unbelieving, both among the Jews and Gentiles,—in hardening their hearts against God's call, and so thrusting salvation from them,—cannot escape the judicial vengeance wherewith God will visit them that do despite unto the Spirit of grace by rejecting His proffered mercy in the blood of His Son, when and wherever He causes His gospel to be preached. What the Apostle writes in the first three chapters of the Romans he amply experienced in the course of his apostolical labour. The preaching of God's Word was no sham-fight with him, penetrated as he was by the conviction, that whether it be to life or to death, "God always causeth the heralds of His salvation to triumph in Christ," (2 Cor. ii. 14, &c.) And that he knew the import of the curse over a city which rejects the message of peace, he shews by following Christ's command, (Matt. x. 14,) in shaking off the dust of his feet against them at Antioch who would rather allow themselves to be led away by the false Jews to persecution than by the true Israelite to the following of Jesus, (Acts xiii. 50, 51.)

Lamenting over the obdurate hardness and sad fate of his nation, who were "filling up their sins alway," and drawing God's "wrath upon them to the uttermost," by hindering the Gentiles to be saved, (1 Thess. ii. 16,) Paul proceeded with Barnabas to Iconium, where, alas! they met with still greater opposition. Here again they entered the synagogue, and "so spake, that a great multitude both of the Jews and also of the Greeks believed;" and "the Lord gave testimony unto the word of His grace by granting signs and wonders to be done by their hands." But here also "the unbelieving Jews stirred up the Gentiles," and when there was an assault made upon them by both, they fled—not back, however, but forward into the Lycaonian cities, preaching the same Gospel, which everywhere causes so wholesome a stir, (Acts xiv. 1–7.) At Lystra we find the Apostle growing like a palm under her lofty load. A miracle, wrought after the manner of Peter's at the temple gate, hurried away the populace to the enthusiastic exclamation, "The gods are come down to us in the likeness of men;" and the crafty town-priest of Jupiter, seeing his consequence at stake, quickly "brought oxen and garlands unto the gate," to do them homage by a sacrifice. "Chafed at such dignity right sore," the two "mortal men," who of themselves would be no better than the meanest of the blind heathen, "ran in among the people," and Paul seized upon their hearts with all the power of his soul-winning love and heavenly wisdom. He feels himself standing on a cross-way of time. The living God, who made heaven and earth, hath in times past suffered all Gentile nations to walk in their own ways; yet of His being *their* God also, (Rom. iii. 29,) He hath not left Himself without witness; and the Lycaonians, whose fruitful fields were the granaries of Asia Minor, heard this day proclaimed before their delighted ears the name of the true God, as their heavenly Nourisher and the Filler of their "hearts with food and gladness." "And with these sayings scarce restrained they the people, that they had not done sacrifice unto them." Nevertheless, here also they were not "delivered from unreasonable and wicked men: for all men have not faith," (2 Thess. iii. 2;) and after a while Paul lay bruised and smarting under the stones of the Jews, who came thither from Antioch and Iconium to destroy the work of God; and the Lycaonians had no further fancy for the two "mortal men," who, though healing their impotent cripple, could not shield themselves from the stones of the Jews. Howbeit, some of the new disciples—Timothy was probably one of them, (Acts xvi. 1)—surmounted the blow; for not in Paul, but in Jesus they believed. And as these stood round about Paul, "supposing he had been dead," this servant of the most high God, chafed at oxen and garlands, but bearing stones patiently, rose up and returned undaunted into the city, (Acts xiv. 8-20.)

Next day they came to Derbe, and having preached the Gospel to that city also, and taught many, they retraced their way, content for the present with the gospel breastwork they had reared in the four cities, Antioch, Iconium, Lystra, and Derbe, and "confirming," as they repassed them, "the souls of the disciples, exhorting them to continue in the faith, and that we"—*i.e.*, all who with Paul live a life of faith in Jesus—"must through much tribulation enter into the kingdom of God." Far from being discouraged at the ill success of this first missionary tour, the Apostle would anticipate with fondest hope a bright harvest from the many tender "blades" springing here and there over all the ground they had trod. To consolidate their work, and commit the newly-gathered disciples to the care of the Lord, they ordained them elders in every church, and returned by way of Perga and Attalia to Antioch, "whence they had been recommended to the grace of God for the work which they fulfilled;" and having gathered the Church together, they rehearsed all that God had done with them, and how He had opened the door of faith unto the Gentiles, (Acts xiv. 21-27.) Thus the Apostle laid all honour humbly at the Lord's feet in His Church,— the keeper of His counsel and dispenser of His grace by the Holy Ghost,—forming, at the same time, a bond of union between the mother Church and her newly-born daughters.

A twofold danger, which now began to threaten the young churches gathered from amongst Jews and Gentiles, —by either the former narrowing the door of faith, or the latter widening that of Christian life,—was averted by the apostolical synod at Jerusalem, under the guidance of the Holy Ghost. Being chosen with Barnabas to represent the Antiochian church there, Paul, for the sake of peace, willingly bore the appearance of dependence upon those "who seemed to be pillars," (Gal. ii. 9,) a proof of self-denial for which the Lord strengthened him by a special revelation, (ib. ver. 2.) But the viewing of Paul's character in the light of the Jerusalem synod, we reserve for the closing chapter of this sketch.

Before setting out on his second missionary tour, Paul parted from Barnabas. In their contention about Mark, the old Saul seems to have had his share. But the Lord covered the fault of His faithful servant, and knew how to convert it into good. In full independence he now entered upon his high work, choosing Silas for his companion, one of those deputed by the Jerusalem synod to Antioch, whose blessed footsteps proved that Paul had chosen the right man, (Acts xv. 36-40.) Besides him, he also chose Timothy, whom he found at Lystra, grown, since his first visit, into good report among the brethren there. In this youth, whom he took to his heart with tender love, he won his most faithful companion, whose unselfish mind resembled his own in entire devotion to the work of the Lord, (Phil. ii. 20.) A bosom friend he proved to him, such as Paul Gerhard prayed for, when he sang, "According to thy will give me a friend, in whose fidelity my heart may find repose." From the very first St Paul evinces a confidence in his genuine faith, which is most creditable to Timothy. While he would not circumcise Titus, because of false brethren, (Gal. ii. 3, 4,) he circumcised Timothy in forbearance with the weakness of the Jews, (Acts xvi. 3;) and he felt able to do so, because he knew him to be so freed by faith from subjection to ordinances, that without danger to his Christ-betrothed soul, Timothy, for the sake of others, could waive in this instance his liberty in Christ. This virtue of acting under all circumstances as "the Lord's freeman," (1 Cor. vii. 22,) was most prominent in Paul himself, as hereafter we shall have occasion to see. A third coadjutor in the Apostle's work, whom the Lord had designed to become the interpreter of the history himself henceforth witnessed, was St Luke the Evangelist, who, without noticing his name, modestly intimates his companionship of the Apostle by speaking, from Acts xvi. 10, onward, in the first person.* Cf. Acts xvi. 1-3.

The wings of the dove had waxed strong for a flight abroad, and being "forbidden by the Holy Ghost to preach the word in Asia," St Paul pressed forward to the West. Close before the door of Europe—at Troas—there appeared to him an angel, in the form of "a man of Macedonia," whose cry for help gave expression to the mute misery of the heathen there. Manned with such helpful hands, the ship soon gained the Macedonian harbour, Neapolis, whence at once they proceeded to the principal free city, Philippi,

* Except from the Apostle's departure from Philippi, (Acts xvi. 40,) to his return to it, (Acts xx. 6,) a space of about half a dozen years, during which time Luke seems to have remained in that city.—TR.

where Imperial Rome held her sway, and was now for the first time* ominously met by the heralds of a mightier kingdom, that of Christ. With Lydia, whose heart the Lord opened, and with her household, the first Christian church in Europe began. But "the strong man armed," seeing "his palace" beset, and his peace disturbed, stirred up the greedy masters of "a certain damsel possessed with the spirit of divination," and they accused the apostles before the magistrates, as troublers of their city and teachers of anti-Roman customs; whereupon they were beaten and cast into prison. There, with "their feet made fast in the stocks," Paul and Silas prayed and sang midnight praises unto God, rejoicing in their tribulation for Christ's sake. And the Lord gave His echo to their prayer in a great earthquake shaking the foundations of the prison; "and immediately all the doors were opened, and every one's bands were loosed." But the salvation of one soul—that of the terror-stricken jailer—far outweighed, in Paul's estimation, their own stocks and bands; and a second family was won that night to the faith of the Lord Jesus. "Thou shalt be saved, and thy house," said the Apostle, not sparing the health-giving water of the "fountain opened" in Christ "for sin and for uncleanness," (Zech. xiii. 1.) The manner of their release from prison shews us a trait of that wisdom which Paul knew how to use for the benefit of the Church of Christ. The magistrates, apprehensive of having acted illegally in their imprisonment, now wished to push them off quietly. Against this Paul entered his protest, and his appeal for justice to the privilege of a Roman citizen (*civis Romanus sum*) brought the perplexed city prætors themselves to the prison, beseeching the apostles themselves to come out and leave the city. "All things

---

* At least in Europe.—Tr.

are yours," (1 Cor. iii. 22,) even citizenships and privileges in this world; which in this instance served the cause of the Church's temporal well-being at Philippi. Singing praises in bands and the stocks, from which a miraculous earthquake set them free, Paul was yet sober enough to claim the rightful protection of legal authority; and what here he did is but the prelude of the practical comment which his life, down to his appeal to Cæsar, furnishes to his own teaching of the blessings of civil authorities, as "the powers ordained of God," (Rom. xiii. 1-6.) Cf. Acts xvi. 6, &c.

At Thessalonica, the capital of Macedonia, "a great multitude of devout Greeks, and of the chief women not a few, consorted with Paul and Silas;" not, however, without again provoking the envy of the Jews, who here had their principal synagogue; and by stirring up "certain lewd fellows of the baser sort," who "set all the city in an uproar," they caused the apostles to be sent away by night. As those of Jerusalem had accused Jesus, so these accused His servants, of opposition to Cæsar. But He who gave Pilate power that the Shepherd should be smitten instead of the sheep, here inclined the rulers of the city to "let these go." Thus Paul and Silas escaped from the house of Jason unto Berea. But how does the Apostle leave his new-born children at Thessalonica? Though not without anxiety, for the tempter lay at their door, (1 Thess. iii. 5,) yet with a gladness at their already proved patience in suffering, which makes him exclaim, "Ye are our glory and joy," (1 Thess. ii. 14-20.) From Acts xvii. 10, it would appear that Paul left Timothy for a while at Thessalonica. At Berea the Lord refreshed the soul of His hard-toiling labourer; for here the Jews "were more noble than those at Thessalonica, in that they received the word with all readiness of mind, and searched the Scriptures daily, whether those things were so." Yet not long was he to enjoy this rare delight in his own people. Indeed, enjoying —even in this noblest sense—was, throughout, less the motto of his life than self-denying toil. The Jews from Thessalonica came thither also, and stirred up the people against the word "preached of Paul," who, much as it went against his undaunted nature to flee, yet, since this served to bring fruit unto the Lord, went "as it were to the sea," and came to Athens, leaving Silas and Timothy (who had meanwhile come from Thessalonica) still at Berea. Cf. Acts xvii. 1-15.

While waiting here for his companions, Paul passed lonely through the world-famed city of wisdom, "the Altar of the Greeks and their Guildhall, and of all Arts and Sciences the Cradle." Not insensible to the Athenians' taste for the beautiful, so profusely displayed in the sculptured representations of their deities, yet his "spirit was stirred" in him when he saw the city wholly given to idolatry. Poignant woe over the glittering wretchedness of the ignorant and yet wisdom-proud Greeks, and holy zeal against *him*, who had guided with seductive hand their chisel in the masterpieces of human art, moved the Apostle's soul. But that "the spirits of the prophets are subject to the prophets," (1 Cor. xiv. 32,) he signally evinced here. Unprovoked by the loose talk of the Epicureans and the supercilious mockery of the Stoics, he allowed himself to be led to the Areopagus; whence, surveying the town with all its splendid symbols of idolatrous worship, he would grieve in his mind over "the truth of God being changed into a lie, and the creature worshipped and served more than the Creator, who is blessed for ever," (Rom. i. 25.) He gladly bore to be looked upon by the curious Athenians as "a setter forth of strange gods," and with the quick eye of love, which made him "all things to all men," (1 Cor. ix. 22,) he looked about him for a way of access to the hearts of a people, to whom "Christ crucified" was "foolishness," (1 Cor. i. 23.) All excitement of feeling he knew how to subject to his will in the Lord; every word is well weighed in the balance of love, and adapted to the state of his hearers. He takes his starting point from an inscription he had read on one of their altars: "To the unknown God." Fain to discover in this confession of their ignorance an unstilled sigh after truth, he declares to them that God whom they ignorantly worship, as the Lord of heaven and earth, who is throned in blissful independence,—needeth nothing of men, but giveth them all things, and so directeth all their ways, by demonstrations both of His wrath and mercy, as to lead them to seek Him, "if haply they might feel after Him and find Him" to be their Creator and kind Preserver,—who, instead of rejecting and destroying man's corrupt nature, has reserved it to verify the saying of their poets, "we are His offspring," but in a higher sense than theirs—viz., in the Christian sentiments of those who shall have found God, not in the likeness of any phantom of the human imagination, but in that *one man* whom He hath ordained to judge the world, even in the man Christ Jesus. To Him the Apostle knows finally how to direct the hearts of the Athenians, that now, after God hath "winked at the time of their ignorance," they may repent, in order to escape the already appointed day of judgment; on which He whom God hath raised from the dead, and whom Paul now preaches to them, "will judge the world in righteousness." Thus the Apostle spake at Athens, but the seed, alas! fell mostly on hard-trodden ground "by the wayside." With mockery over the resurrection of the dead on the one side, and on the other with civil promises to hear more of it another time, the irksome preacher was got rid of—unmolested, but unsought. "Not many wise men," (1 Cor. i. 26;) howbeit a few "clave unto him, and believed;" and Paul deemed not his strength spent in vain, but rather as amply repaid, in the salvation of a noted "Dionysius," a less noted "Damaris," "and others with them." Cf. Acts xvii. 16-34.

Nevertheless, Paul quitted Athens in great heaviness. We should certainly form a very untrue picture of this holy labourer of Christ, were we to impute to him a stoical equanimity. Hot ran the blood in his veins. He was ardent both in his love and grief. On his arrival at Corinth from Athens he was "in weakness, and in fear, and in much trembling," (1 Cor. ii. 3.) His indifferent reception at Athens augured but ill for him in voluptuous Corinth, where Grecian philosophy vied with Roman greatness, where lewdness, shameless and refined, abounded, with mammon, luxury, and fashion. Here he entirely abstained from meeting, as he had done at Athens, the "wise" Greeks with the weapons of their own human wisdom; but knowing "the foolishness of God to be wiser than men," and content to win but those whom God hath chosen,—the base and despised of the world, (1 Cor. i. 25-29,)—he "determined not to know anything among them, save Jesus Christ and Him crucified," (1 Cor. ii. 2.) Being received by Aquila and Priscilla, Jewish exiles from Rome, he wrought with them as tentmaker, only attending and reasoning with Jews and Greeks in the synagogue every Sabbath. On the arrival, however, of Silas and Timothy from Macedonia, "Paul was pressed in the spirit, and testified to the Jews that Jesus was Christ," having been greatly refreshed by the news which Timothy—whom he had sent back from Athens to Thessalonica—brought him from the congregation there, (cf. 1 Thess. iii.) "For now," he writes, (ver. 8,) in this very first of his apostolical epistles,—bequeathing to the Church of all times his apostolical labour,—now "we live, if ye stand fast in the Lord." What importance he attaches to this branch of his apostolic office,—the Epistles,—we see from his solemn admonition at the close of this: "I charge you by the Lord that this epistle be read unto all the holy brethren," (chap. v. 27, cf., in the second epistle, written shortly after, chap. ii. 15.) From the opposing and blaspheming Jews Paul turned, "free from their blood," unto the Gentiles, and had the pleasure to be followed by Crispus, the chief ruler of the synagogue, whom he baptized with his own hand, (1 Cor. i. 14,) into the house of the God-fearing Gentile Justus, where the rising Christian church assembled, to the ministry of which Stephanas devoted himself, who, with his house, became "the first-fruits of Achaia," (1 Cor. xvi. 15.) Apprehensive of his speedy expulsion from them, the Apostle might naturally tremble for his little flock of saints in a city intoxicated with worldly pleasures, when the Lord strengthened him by a vision, shewing him "the measure" of His rule, a measure to reach even unto Corinth, (2 Cor. x. 13,) and bidding him to "speak, and not hold his peace; for that no man should hurt him, and that He had much people in this city." How, thereupon, he continued his ministry, teaching the word of God among them, is seen by a glance at his Epistles to the Corinthians. "I have fed you with milk," he says, "and not with meat; for hitherto ye were not able to bear it," (1 Cor. iii. 2;) yet by this milk of the Gospel they not only were saved, if they believed in Christ dying for our sins and rising again according to the Scriptures, (1 Cor. xv. 1-4,) but were likewise "enriched in everything by Christ, in all utterance and in all knowledge," (1 Cor. i. 5.) Not seeking his own profit, but that of many, that they may be saved (1 Cor. x. 33,) was the Apostle's rule of life, and the testimony of his conscience everywhere, but "more abundantly," he says, "to you-ward," (2 Cor. i. 12,) who "are in our hearts to live and die with you," (2 Cor. vii. 3.) "I have espoused you to one husband," he declares in another place, "that I may present you as a chaste virgin to Christ," (2 Cor. xi. 2;) and, lo! the Church of God at Corinth became a focus for the saints in all Achaia, (2 Cor. i. 1,) the seal of Paul's apostleship in the Lord, (1 Cor. ix. 2,) "the epistle of Christ," written in his heart, not with ink, but with the Spirit of the living God, and known and read of all men, (2 Cor. iii. 2, 3.) This epistle the unbelieving Jews at Corinth could also read, either as a bill of indictment against, or a "still small voice" for them. But they sought to convert Gallio, the deputy of Achaia, into a Pilate. However, Gallio would have nothing to do with their "question of words," and drove them from his judgment-seat. Thus, under the protection of a heathen magistrate, who—"caring for none of those things"—was simply guided by a sense of legal right, Paul was enabled, "as a wise master-builder," to lay the foundation, (1 Cor. iii. 10,) and to plant what afterwards was to be watered by Apollos, (ib. ver. 6,) whose peculiar talents for the work the Apostle appreciates with unenvious satisfaction. Cf. Acts xviii. 1-17.

Ere we follow the Apostle to Ephesus, we must view him yet on leaving Corinth. As he embarked at Cenchrea, "he shaved his head; for he had a vow," (Acts xviii. 18.) Thus "the Lord's freeman" would willingly put himself under the restraint of a vow, till his work at Corinth should be completed; for till then he had doubtless vowed to the Lord, that he would let his hair grow,* (Numb. vi. 5.)

---

* I have heard of a pious youth forcing himself to a lengthened seclusion from the world by a vow, that he would not have his hair cut till he should have studied through the whole Bible in the original; and it was said he kept the vow.—TR.

Behold this evangelical Nazarite! What in Acts xxi. 24 he submitted to for the Jews' sake, he did of free choice at Corinth, for his own and his work's sake. The symbol of a man's honour (1 Cor. xi. 3-15) he laid at the Lord's feet, to have this mark of a Nazarite always remind him of his utter dependence on God's all-sufficient power to make him an able minister of the New Testament, for his work here at Corinth, (2 Cor. iii. 5, 6.) Thus the Apostle knew how to breathe a spirit of life derived from Christ into the "beggarly elements" of the law; not he served them, but they him, unto Apostolic power in Pauline weakness.

At Ephesus, the capital of Grecian Asia Minor, the Apostle left Priscilla and Aquila,—no mean gift, for they became his fellow-helpers in Christ Jesus," (Rom. xvi. 3,)— while himself hasted thence to Jerusalem to convey to the mother Church the salutations of her many children, as the best Pentecostal offering for the ensuing feast. A beautiful Christian realisation this of the prophetic signs given on the day of Pentecost. For the "house of prayer for all people," (Isa. lvi. 7,) whose empty form remained yet but a while on Mount Zion, was now growing up apace—a new spiritual house—under the blessed hands of the apostolic master-builder, (Acts xviii., xix., &c.)

"If God will," was Paul's modest reply to the Jews at Ephesus, who for once "desired him to tarry,"—"if God will, I will return again unto you;" and God willed it. At Antioch, whither now for the last time he returned, he met with Peter,\* whom he openly blamed for dissembling with the Jews, (Gal. ii. 11, &c., cf. vi. 1.) Travelling through Galatia and Phrygia "in order," and "strengthening," as he passed along, "all the disciples," who ever and anon

---

\* This meeting, it would seem, from Barnabas being mentioned in connexion with it, (Gal. ii. 13,) took place during a former stay of Paul and Barnabas together at Antioch, (Acts xv. 35.)—TR.

were troubled by legal Judaizers, the Apostle again reached Ephesus, which was destined to become the golden link between the churches of the East and West. Twelve Pentecostal sheaves (Acts xix. 1-7) he was permitted here to glean for the Holy Ghost; and when constrained by divers hardened and unbelieving Jews to leave their synagogue, ("Behold your house is left unto you desolate," Luke xiii. 35,) he preached the Gospel for two years in the learned school of Tyrannus, whither both Jews and Greeks from far and near resorted, (Eph. ii. 11, &c.;) "so that all they which dwelt in Asia heard the word of the Lord Jesus," and Ephesus became a mother church to those at Colosse, Laodicea, and Hierapolis. Thus the Apostle had planted twelve churches, when—standing upon the meridian of his missionary career—he said, " I must also see Rome." Ephesus was a mart for magic, and God, through the work of His servant, and through the "special miracles" He wrought by his hands, held judgment over the gods of Greece, causing many of the believers, who hitherto had "used curious arts," at once so thoroughly to purge their dwellings of them, that they brought together their books of sorcery, to the amount of "50,000 pieces of silver," (about £2000, at which they had bought them,) "and burned them before all men." After what manner the Apostle spent the "two years" among them, is shewn by his valedictory address to their elders, (Acts xx. 18-35.) Twice he reminds them of his tears in seeking to win every one's soul. He indeed, says Chrysostom, "watered with his tears the seed he sowed," and therefore also "he came again with joy, and brought his sheaves with him." Manliness was a fundamental feature both in his natural and sanctified character, (cf. 1 Cor. xvi. 13.) Therefore his manly tears must have fallen hot into the souls he sought to gain, (cf. Phil. iii. 18.) "Weeping goes before working, and suffering before doing," says Luther, who in manliness of mind was Paul's counterpart. And the indefatigable labourer who wrung from his feeble body the exertions of the ministerial workman under pain and temptation, who ceased not from warning and teaching, both publicly and from house to house, devoting to it even the night, as the day grew too short for him;—this "worker together with God" would yet work also with his hands as tentmaker, and thus eat his own bread in the sweat of his brow. "I have shewed you all things," he could say, "how that so labouring ye ought to support the weak; and to remember the words of the Lord Jesus, how He said, It is more blessed to give than to receive." If the Apostle wrote his First Epistle to Timothy upon a visitation-visit through Macedonia to Corinth (2 Cor. xii. 14, xiii. 1, 2) about this time, (which from 1 Tim. iii. 14, iv. 13, seems probable,) his pastoral exhortations in that epistle would point to a special cause for his tears. Not all the members of the Ephesian church would content themselves with his teaching "that which is good to the use of edifying," but some would still cleave to "fables and genealogies," and in spiritual pride of heart affect to know secrets, whereby faith would sicken and love grow cold, (1 Tim. i. 4-7, iv. 7, vi. 20, 21.) This solicitude about the Ephesians he bore in his heart, together with the far deeper grief about the Galatians, whose "enemy" he had become, as their false teachers would make them believe, and "of whom he travailed in birth again," (Gal. iv. 18, 19,) while at Ephesus; for there he (doubtless) wrote this Epistle, wherein, both against their legal false teachers and the spurious work-mongers of all times, he declares his heaven-revealed Gospel of Christ as the one, beside which there is not another. And still a third sorrow came upon him about this time. Already he had sent away Timothy and Erastus into Macedonia, to gather the collection for the poor saints at Jerusalem, (1 Cor. xvi. 1, &c.,) when intelligence reached him from the Corinthian church, which called for his first epistle to them. An Easter epistle it has been appropriately called. In view of that approaching feast, he exhorts them to purge out the old leaven of malice, (1 Cor. v. 6-8,) reproving their lukewarmness and disregard of wholesome church-discipline, and further blaming them for overrating spiritual gifts in their greedy eagerness for inflating knowledge. Yet while his words at times run like rolling thunder over the heads of the ungrateful Corinthians, how like a stream runs through this very epistle his Christian love, and how worthy of being served with the mysteries of God does he count His church at Corinth! And all this, while at Ephesus he had to fight with "beasts," (1 Cor. xv. 32,) at Satan's instigation, who—bent on his destruction—caused him to be treated "as the filth of the world, and the offscouring of all things" (1 Cor. iv. 13,) because that "a great door and effectual was opened unto him at Ephesus," (1 Cor. xvi. 8, 9.) Yet, unmindful of personal danger, he was only solicitous to preserve from spiritual harm the imperilled members of his scattered flocks. Daily pressed upon by the care of all the churches, he exclaims: "Who is weak, and I am not weak? who is offended, and I burn not?" (2 Cor. xi. 28, 29.) For the wellbeing of the church at Crete likewise he cared in these troublous days, by his Epistle to Titus, written probably about the same time. In the tumult raised at Ephesus in defence of Diana and her silversmiths, whose craft was in danger, the Lord shielded His servant—as aforetime in Thessalonica—from the rage of an excited populace, through the friendly counsel of "certain of the chief of Asia," and according to Rom. xvi. 4, also by Priscilla and Aquila risking their lives for him; but withal it was again the arm of legal, though heathen authority, which here, as at Corinth, went to restrain the evil-doers; for although the town-clerk had to throw his official shield over the Ephesians' "great goddess Diana," yet he referred Demetrius and his fellow-craftsmen to the open law, and warned the people against the "danger of being called in question for this day's uproar." Thus graciously did the Lord answer the prayers of His people, "for kings and all that are in authority," (1 Tim. ii. 2,) and made their meek submission, according to the Apostle's doctrine and example, (Tit. iii. 1, 2,) redound to their own benefit and protection under persecution. (Cf. Acts xix.)

Pentecost, till which time Paul desired to tarry at Ephesus, (1 Cor. xvi. 8,) was fast approaching, and the Church was again in peace. Like one raised from the dead, he stood among his brethren, (2 Cor. i. 8-11.) Abundantly comforted by the unlooked-for happy termination of the uproar, he once more called unto him the disciples, and embracing them, departed for Macedonia, (Acts xx. 1.) He made his first halt at Troas, where a door to preach the Gospel was opened unto him of the Lord. But "I had no rest in my spirit," he writes, "because I found not Titus my brother," (2 Cor. ii. 12, 13.) What hurried him thus restless from Troas's open door? He had sent Titus to relieve Timothy at Corinth. How could he remain quiet at Troas, while ruin was menacing his vineyard at Corinth? These sad apprehensions about them followed him to Macedonia; "for, when we were come into Macedonia," he again writes, "our flesh had no rest, but we were troubled on every side: without were fightings, within were fears," (2 Cor. vii. 5.) In Macedonia, however, where the Church flourished in fair spiritual beauty (2 Cor. viii.,) he met Timothy with good news from Corinth, which made him at once begin to write to his beloved Corinthians a second time. Thereupon, shortly after, Titus also arrived, whose more recent glad tidings about them made him abound in joy: "O ye Corinthians, our mouth is enlarged," (2 Cor. vi. 11;) "God, that comforteth those that are cast down, comforted us by the coming of Titus," (2 Cor. vii. 6;) for he told Paul and Timothy of the Corinthians' "earnest desire," of their "mourning," and their "fervent mind" toward the Apostle, whom they had grieved. Of all epistles, this paints the Apostle most clearly before our eyes. "With many tears" he had written his first letter, (2 Cor. ii. 4;) and in this second one, too, the Corinthians could not fail to see the traces of his moistened eyes. "I trust," says the faithful shepherd—whom the Lord never permits to become an hireling—"I trust ye shall acknowledge even to the end, as also ye have acknowledged us in part, that we are your rejoicing, even as ye also are ours in the day of the Lord Jesus," (2 Cor. i. 13, 14.) His heart so thrills with emotions in "longing" after them, "for the exceeding grace of God in them," and so exults in the glory of his apostolic office, which God enables him faithfully to discharge, that he can hardly find utterance for the thoughts that rush in upon his mind like flashes of lightning, and he strains every nerve to give expression to the inexpressible love his spirit breathes.

Having penetrated to Illyricum, (Rom. xv. 19,) the Apostle wintered three months in Greece, (Acts xx. 1-3,) and Gaius of Derbe became his host at Corinth, (Rom. xvi. 23.) This period is marked by a double labour of love, answering to the twofold magnet by which he was drawn. It was now that he completed the long-desired collection for the poor saints at Jerusalem; thereby forming a bond of peaceful union between the mother and her daughter churches, which might well have attracted the unbelieving Jews to Zion's beauty, (cf. 2 Cor. viii. and ix., and Rom. xv.

25, &c.;) and it was here he wrote to the Romans that pearl of all his epistles, which evinces the Church of Christ in that city to be indeed the fruit of his apostolic labour, although he had not as yet reached it in person, (Rom. xv. 22, &c.;) for it stamps his seal upon "that form of doctrine," (Rom. vi. 17) which, not through "another man's," (Rom. xv. 20,) but his own labour, had been delivered to them—viz., through those several evangelic messengers, whose "beautiful" footsteps had preceded him thither with the message of his apostolical preaching, (cf. Rom. xvi.) "More boldly" (Rom. xv. 15) does his spirit soar in this than any other of his epistles, testifying to the Church in that capital of the world, that he is not ashamed of the Gospel of Christ, inasmuch as "it is the power of God unto salvation to every one that believeth; to the Jew first, and also to the Greek," (Rom. i. 16.) There falls the hammer of his heavenly dialectic power with crushing force upon man's corruption, till all boasting is excluded, (Rom. iii. 27,) and the blows of his forcible logic lay the creature and her reason prostrate in the dust before God, (Rom. ix. 20.) Most prominent in this epistle is the peculiar sequence of his thoughts, forming—as an able judge expresses it—"a strong tissue woven of sinews and muscles, a living string of ramified tendons, like the rows of pillars and arches in a Gothic cathedral, or like one of Handel's grand fugues." The boldness with which he writes, and which at times excites even his own humble gaze, we learn to understand, if we bear in mind the historical standing-place from whence he writes. Set at large out of narrow straits, led from depths up to a lofty height, there stands the great Apostle of the Gentiles at Corinth, looking, as from the summit of a mountain, back eastwards to Jerusalem, forward into the west—to Rome, and beyond it into Spain. As far as to Illyricum he has spread the Gospel-net, and built up the evangelical altar, upon which the Gentiles, sanctified through the Holy Ghost, are being offered unto God a sweet savour of Christ. His prophetic eye already views the church at Rome as heiress to that of Jerusalem; and, clad in the bright armour of his strong knowledge, he brings to bear all the experience of his heaven-taught wisdom on the service of God in the Gospel of His Son, (Rom. i. 9,) which is also "*his* gospel," (Rom. xvi. 25,) in order so to strengthen and consolidate that Church—of Jew and Gentile joined in *One*,—that she might become a pillar of the One, Holy, Catholic, and Apostolic Church. And though her candlestick has been removed out of its place, here, in Paul's epistle, it stands unshaken, and sheds through the universe its inextinguishable light. Where its doctrine reigns, there is Rome's and Jerusalem's legitimate heiress. An Erasmus, with a shrug of his shoulder, could utter the wanton word: "The abstruseness of the Roman epistle excels its utility;" but Luther called it the Lord's lantern, illuminating all the chambers of Holy Writ. Thanks be to God for this truest bulwark of the Gospel, this choicest flower of Paul's evangelical labour, a very amaranth, unfading and immortal! Amen.

> " Strive, when thou art call'd of God,
> When He draws thee by His grace,
> Strive to cast away the load
> That would clog thee in the race.
>
> " Fight, though it may cost thy life;
> Storm the kingdom, but prevail;
> Let not Satan's fiercest strife,
> Make thy heart to faint or quail.
>
> " Wrestle, till through every vein,
> Love and strength are glowing warm :
> Paul's love could the world disdain,
> Half-love will not bide the storm."[*]

---

[*] In these and other verses in the remaining chapters, I have mostly followed the " Lyra Germanica."—Tr.

## VI.

## THE PRISONER OF JESUS CHRIST.

*"Being such an one as Paul the aged, and now also a prisoner of Jesus Christ."*—PHILEM. 9.

ERE the Apostle was bound "in bonds," (Eph. vi. 20,) he was bound in the spirit:—

> " O Love! who thus hast bound me fast
> Beneath that gentle yoke of Thine;
> Love, who hast conquer'd me at last,
> And rapt away this heart of mine;
> O Love! I give myself to Thee,
> Thine ever, only Thine to be."

Thus it sounded in Paul's soul ever since the day that he became "the won of the Lord Jesus." To do nothing against, but all for the truth, (2 Cor. xiii. 8;) to "suffer"—not as an evil-doer, but for Christ's sake—" even unto bonds," (2 Tim. ii. 9;) to be made a spectacle unto the world, and to angels, and to men; yea, and to become a fool, if it be but for Christ's sake, (1 Cor. iv. 9, 10;) such was the mind of " the prisoner of Jesus Christ," unto whom the world was crucified by Christ, and he unto the world, (Gal. vi. 14.) A true bondman of Christ he was, who bore in his body the marks of the Lord Jesus, (Gal. vi. 17.) Thus not spiritually only, but also bodily it pleased the Lord to call His servant to the state of a bondman; and with what patience, nay, even exultation, did the Apostle bear these bonds of his, as an order of honour to him, and a glory to Christ's Church, (Eph. iii. 13.) The remembrance of Peter's falling chains* (Acts xii. 7) is hardly so glorious and so edifying as that of St Paul rejoicing in his chains, and triumphing over all enemies, as shewn in his last five Epistles, and the last eight chapters of the Acts.

Where the Apostle speaks to the Romans of his purposed journey to Jerusalem, there he also beseeches them to strive together with him in their prayers to God for him, that he may "be delivered from them that do not believe in Judæa," and that his service may be accepted of the saints at Jerusalem, (Rom. xv. 25-31.) A service of love truly this journey was. Surrounded by the first-fruits of his harvest among the Gentiles, seven in number, (Acts xx. 4,) he embarked for Asia, bearing in his ministering hands tokens of sympathy and love from his heathen converts to those of the true Israel at Jerusalem. When Jesus held His royal entry into Jerusalem, there were certain Greeks who desired to see Him, before whom and the still enthusiastic multitude the Lord spoke that inimitable word about the corn of wheat that must fall into the ground and die ere it can bring forth fruit. Now this was accomplished, and Paul brought the first-fruits of the Lord to Jerusalem. "If any man serve me, let him follow me," continued Christ, and His servant Paul followed Him on the way of self-devotion even unto death. His journey to Jerusalem bears indeed some resemblance to that which the church calls on us to remember on every Sunday before Lent:— "Behold we go up to Jerusalem," (Luke xviii. 31.) He that raised Lazarus is drawn by the cords of love to go as a lamb to the slaughter; he that raised Eutychus by the power of Christ, is drawn after Him by the power of His love. Well might Paul, over the eucharistic table at Troas, continue his speech till midnight, (Acts xx. 7;) for they

---

* Celebrated by the Roman Catholics on their so-called "Lammas-day," (1st of August.)

were parting words inspired by the Comforter, in view of his way of suffering; and in his solitary walk "afoot" from Troas to Assos (ib. ver. 13) he still strengthened his soul in God, while, like his heavenly Master, "he steadfastly set his face to Jerusalem." "And now," he says to the Ephesian elders at Miletus, "behold, I go bound in the spirit unto Jerusalem, not knowing the things that shall befall me there: save that the Holy Ghost witnesseth in every city, saying that bonds and afflictions abide me." That he expected the eve of his labour drawing nigh, and spoke in view of his approaching martyrdom, this we feel through the whole of that valedictory address, at which we have already before taken occasion to glance. Under the cross-predicting witness of the Holy Ghost, he departs hence, with only this object in view, to "finish his course with joy, and to testify the Gospel of the grace of God," if by any means—whether by word or deed, preaching or suffering—he might provoke to emulation them which are his flesh, and might save some of them, (Rom. xi. 14;) a true Benjamite, he was still bent on "dividing the spoil at night," (Gen. xlix. 29,) even in Jerusalem. By enjoining them to take heed to the flock, over which the Holy Ghost had made them overseers, and to watch against the "grievous wolves," which after his departure would enter in among them, "not sparing the flock,"—Paul made his testament with the elders of the Ephesian church. Yea, and he told them openly, "Behold, I know that ye all, among whom I have gone preaching the kingdom of God, shall see my face no more." This "I know" seems to contradict a later "knowing" of the Apostle. "Having this confidence," he writes to the Philippians from Rome, "I know that I shall abide and continue with you all for your furtherance and joy of faith," (Phil. i. 25;) and in this confidence he asks the Colossian Philemon (ver. 22) to prepare him a lodging. But what is contradictory to reason is edifying to faith. The prayers and tears of his flocks have snatched Paul from the jaws of death. The Lord, who heareth prayer, added to his numbered days, as to Hezekiah's aforetime, years still of fruit-working labour. "I trust that through your prayers I shall be given unto you," writes the "prisoner in Christ Jesus" to Philemon. The prayers of the Church formed a fiery wall about the Apostle. His disconsolate children, who there at Miletus all fell on Paul's neck and wept sore, were not to be kept back by his word—that they should see his face no more —from supplicating the Lord for his life; yea, it would make them cry more fervently:—" Notwithstanding, dear Jesus, we beseech Thee, save and preserve unto us our Paul, Thy servant!" It was to incite such prayers in the Church, "for a sweet-smelling savour to God," that the Holy Ghost witnessed of Paul's bonds in every city. (Cf. Acts xx.)

In towns also which his foot had never trod, the Apostle found disciples of Christ, whom he blessed; and they blessed him, for whom he prayed, and they for him. Paul may be bound unto death, but "the word of God is not bound." It shall ride over all the high places of the earth; it shall accomplish that which the Lord pleases, and shall prosper in the thing whereto He sends it; yea, it shall run and be glorified, till all the kingdoms of the earth shall become the kingdoms of God and of His Christ. At Cæsarea Paul entered the house of Philip, the brother evangelist of blessed Stephen, who once had to flee from Jerusalem before Saul's slaughter-breathing spirit, (Acts viii.) Now his four virgin daughters prophesied to Paul of the cross he was so willing to bear. They were joined in this by that Agabus, whose former prophecy had girt the younger Paul for a more joyous journey to Jerusalem,

(Acts xi. 28-30.) To this, his fifth and last, he is also to gird him. "He took Paul's girdle, and bound his own hands and feet, and said, Thus saith the Holy Ghost, So shall the Jews at Jerusalem bind the man that owneth this girdle, and shall deliver him into the hands of the Gentiles." Oft had the Apostle buckled on his girdle, and in all his journeyings among the heathen (2 Cor. xi. 26) had ever borne Jerusalem in his heart. Besides his love for the poor believers there, it was at this time his inextinguishable love for the still poorer unbelievers, which drew him to Jerusalem. And yet at this very time they were going to quench his thirst after their salvation with vinegar, as they had done Christ's upon the cross. His great heaviness and continual sorrow of heart, the desire of his heroic love, wherewith he could wish to purchase his brethren's salvation at the price of his own, (Rom. ix. 1-3,) all was to remain unstilled. Yea, his most ardent affection, instead of melting them, was only going the more to harden and to steel the hearts of his infatuated nation against Jesus, their Saviour. These, and not bodily bonds *alone*, were meant by Agabus's girding. But "Paul the aged" allowed himself to be girded and led, whither Saul the Benjamite would not.

> "If by the light of heavenly grace
> I may but know Thy will,
> And see through doubts and fears Thy face,
> My soul shall hold Thee still.
> Though Thou deniest my heart's best wish,
> I'll not repine, Thy will be mine!
> I have no other will but Thine."

To such fervent aspirations the Lord would draw Paul's soul, when about to pass through his severest trial, that of witnessing Israel's downfall by rejecting her Saviour. Yet to Jerusalem his steps were bent, and whatever ills might betide, it was the Lord's way he went. When, therefore, his best friends, Timothy and Luke included, and doubtless Philip also, his kind host, who well knew Jerusalem and Christ's cross too,—when all, anxious to have his life spared for the Gentiles, besought him with tears not to go up to Jerusalem, then, indeed, he stood there as one that had counted the cost; and severe as might be the struggle against the flesh, crying, "Spare thyself!" Christ gave him the victory, and "Paul answered, What mean ye to weep and to break mine heart? for I am ready, not to be bound only, but also to die at Jerusalem for the name of the Lord Jesus." Ay, whether at Jerusalem or Rome, if it be but for the name of the Lord Jesus, all shall be well. Thus Paul felt, and therefore the most importunate solicitations of his well-meaning and best-beloved brethren in Christ could not wring the cup from his hand. He would pay his vows unto the Lord, (Ps. cxvi. 13-15;) and his original commission ran :—" Bear my name before the Gentiles, and kings, and the children of Israel," (Acts ix. 15.) When Luther was met before Worms by his beloved Spalatin's message, entreating him not to venture into the city, the Lord strengthened him to tread in Paul's footsteps. "The Lord's will be done," said the brethren, and they set out silently toward Jerusalem. They "ceased" their importunities with Paul, but not with the Lord; and His gracious will they obtained, to their unspeakable joy. Soon, indeed, they were to see their beloved teacher, "bound with two chains," in the hands of the Gentiles; but theirs were saving hands; and what they desired for the good of Christ's Church was done, not in spite, but by means of the Apostle's bonds at Jerusalem. Rejoice, then, ye that pray for Zion, and say " Amen " to Paul's doxology —" Unto Him that is able to do exceeding abundantly above all that we ask or think, according to the power that worketh in us, unto Him be glory in the church by Christ

Jesus throughout all ages," (Eph. iii. 20.) Cf. Acts xxi. 1-15.

Accompanied by certain disciples of Cæsarea, Paul entered Jerusalem on the eve, probably, of Pentecost. In order thus best to overcome the prejudices of the dissatisfied Jewish believers, he was with his party warily conducted to the house of Mnason, an old disciple of Cyprus, experienced in the way of the Lord. As he trod the streets of that beloved city, it might sound in his heart, "I will very gladly spend and be spent for you; though the more abundantly I love you, the less I be loved," (2 Cor. xii. 15.) On the following day Paul went to James the Lord's brother, where he met all the elders, and was well received by them. Four years had passed since they last met, and he declared to them one by one what, during this period, God had wrought among the Gentiles by his ministry; "and when they had heard it, they glorified the Lord." These elders, and especially James,—who remained in the darkened city after the other apostles left it,—were lighting the troubled flock with the lamp of life, and to their Christian fidelity the Apostle afterwards bears the highest testimony, (Heb. xiii. 7-17.) It was from respect to them, that he felt himself bound to yield to their request, that he would purify himself, and so satisfy the thousands of prejudiced Jews, just then for the feast at Jerusalem. If they saw with their own eyes that the preacher of evangelical liberty, and of righteousness by faith without works, could also observe the law, where it might do good, would not they be constrained then to open their hearts to this gracious guest visiting the Lord's feast? James and his elders hoped so; and Paul, in the love that "hopeth all things," would willingly become a servant to his weaker brethren in all things lawful. It was not uncommon among the Jews, that poor Nazarites had the temple-costs of their vows defrayed by their wealthier brethren, who thus partook in their services. In this manner Paul was "at charges" with four poor Nazarites. In a more conciliating way he could not have acted. Yet we hear nothing of the effect it produced. But the false Jews, and foremost those of Asia, stirred up the people, and laid hands on him, raising the same cry against him, in which aforetime he also had joined against Stephen; and he would have perished under their murderous hands, had not the Roman soldiers come with all speed to his rescue. No honest Israelite aided him. Thus it was again the heathen authorities to whom he was indebted for protection from the lynch-law of the rabble. Bound with two chains, after Roman custom, he was conveyed to the imperial barracks amid the cries of the mob: —"Away with him!" and up the stairs conducting to the Antonian castle he had to be "borne of the soldiers for the violence of the people." Thus strangely was the saviour of the Gentiles saved by Gentile hands. Yet no sooner did he stand again on his feet, and look down upon the throngs gathered on the slope of the castle, than he resolved to make the top of the stairs his pulpit, and testify to his blind brethren of his happiness, even in bonds, as the won of the Lord Jesus. The Roman chief took him for a notorious Egyptian bandit, who under pretence of being a prophet, had recently fooled thousands of misguided Jews into a revolt against the Roman yoke. But the prisoner's courteous request, in Greek, to be permitted to address the people, astonished the Roman, and still more the civil yet dignified and manly bearing of the ill-treated citizen of Tarsus. He therefore gave him licence to speak. How reproving does this Claudius Lysias stand in front of the raging Jews! and how friendly and significantly did the Lord from heaven beckon to his prisoner, to mark and understand, in whose castle he was secure! (Cf. Acts xxi. 16-40.)

From this time forth, down to its goal,—his arrival at Rome,—the history of the Lord's prisoner is one chain of marvellous deliverances, wrought by explainable means, yet wonderfully providential. That the word of God was not bound, though he was, (2 Tim. ii. 9,) the Apostle now proves in a series of bold defences of the Gospel, for which his very bonds gave him the welcome occasion. Their leading apologetic outlines are:—Jesus of Nazareth is the Christ; Paul, His apostle, is a true Israelite; and the despised sect of the Nazarene is the heir to the promises of God's chosen people. In narrating to the people of Jerusalem the history of his conversion from Pharisaic darkness to the light of Divine grace in Christ Jesus, he smartly knocks at the door of their consciences. He does not spare himself the pain of circumstantially relating what he has been, in order to draw his benighted brethren to become what now he was through grace. With delicate tact, enough to veil from the ear of the Roman soldiers his confessions, as unable to understand them, he spoke in Hebrew. From the heart of the Hebrew his words would best find their way to Hebrew hearts. But theirs were hardened, "according as it is written," (Rom. xi. 8.) A learned disquisition about the relation of their law to the Gospel might have pleased them better. Paul's theology of facts was unbearable to them, they having before determined: "Away with him!" Yet this worn and insignificant-looking man, who "turned the world upside down" by his preaching, knew how to exact silence from them, and "they gave him audience unto that word," wherewith he quoted his commission from Jesus: "Depart, for I will send thee far hence to the Gentiles." This excited their rage. Of the "beds of spices," planted in the garden of the Gentiles by our heavenly Solomon, to provoke by their loveliness his faithless "Shulamite," to return from the wilderness, (Song of Solomon vi. 2-13, viii. 5;)—of the "broken off branches" of their own "olive-tree," making place for the "graffing in among them" of the "wild olive-tree," (Rom. xi.,)—they would hear nothing. They would have stoned him like Stephen, had not the Roman camp been his city of refuge. In the "holy" camp of Israel, now turned into "La-ammi," (Hos. i. 9,) this citizen of the true Israel was doomed to die—in that of the Gentiles, the Roman citizen finds protection under the "powers that be." Cæsar is respected in his camp—the King of Israel despised in that of His people. This tragical event in Paul's life, the preludes to which we saw at Thessalonica and Corinth, is completed here in Jerusalem; and however grating to the Israelite of the tribe of Benjamin, Paul, the prisoner of Jesus Christ, is resigned to it. Yea, recognising in it the Lord's protecting hand, and averse to all straining after martyrdom, he stays the "thongs" and lash of the inquisition, by his resolute appeal to the centurion, (made more timely than aforetime at Philippi:)—"Is it lawful for you to scourge a Roman, and uncondemned?" Cæsar's men understanding his polished Greek better than the Jews their holy Hebrew, Lysias "straightway" had his bands loosed, and commanded the chief priests and all their council to appear before him "on the morrow." (Cf. Acts xxii.)

There, then, stands the Apostle in their midst, a prisoner indeed, but the prisoner of the Lord, only given into Cæsar's custody, who has to serve as "the minister of God to him for good," by procuring him audience. With a quick apprehension of his situation, unprovoked by their treatment, and penetrated only with the desire to omit nothing that might tend to remove the veil from their faces, Paul stood "earnestly beholding the council," and ready for his defence. No one called on him, but the frowning looks of the Pharisees spoke defiance to the renegade; when thus he began: "Men and brethren, I have lived in all good conscience before God until this day." They had thought this former Pharisee must have corrupted and subverted his conscience; but Paul knew all he did to be the doing of the faith of Christ; and therefore, by the grace of God, he could rejoice in the testimony of his conscience, (2 Cor. i. 12.) Now, only, since Christ was born in him, did he serve the God of his fathers with a pure conscience, (2 Tim. i. 3,) and had found that which out of Christ he had sought in vain. Ananias, the high priest, felt the sting of the accusation in Paul's words, and commanded to "smite him on the mouth." Had this drawn from "the choleric" Paul a passionate expression, he still would remain what he is, for a sinless saint he is made only by over-pious bigotry. It being, however, more than improbable, that, by his official dress and his seat of dignity, the Apostle should not have known him to be the high priest, we deem his curse, "God shall smite thee, thou whited wall," not an unwitting sin against God's command, "Thou shalt not curse the ruler of thy people," (Exod. xxii. 28;) and his explanation, "I wist not, brethren, that he was the high priest," not an apology for such sin. It was the putrefaction of Ananias' ungodliness, exhaled from beneath the whitewash of his legal dignity, that made unknowable the bearer of the high-priestly office. Paul looked upon Ananias as God looked upon him, and recognised in him the transgressor of the law, and not the judge after the law.* And, lo, Paul's

* It is with the author's consent, that I express my dissent from his view on this passage—which he has given more at large, and corroborated

address of "brethren" struck upon the hearts of some of the Pharisees, to whom the Sadducees "sitting in Moses' seat" was obnoxious. The presence of mind and serpent-wisdom, wherewith Paul knew how to take advantage of the party-spirit in the council, puts us in mind of Luther's word, "Where grace meets a man, by nature clever and ingenious, it makes use of him for the benefit of others." Paul's sense not unfrequently draws admiration even from worldly people; but they do not think or understand, that Christian Paul acts everywhere, and so here before the council, with all good conscience, always uniting with the serpent-wisdom the harmlessness of the dove, (Matt. x. 16.) His is not the wily shrewdness of a crafty Jew. It was not with the cunning of the lawyer, but the prudence of the pastor, that with the wedge of his timely exclamation—"Men and brethren, I am a Pharisee, the son of a Pharisee, of the hope and resurrection of the dead I am called in question,"—he split into two the hostile camp, which was only kept together by their common enmity to the risen Jesus; and sought to gain over to his faith the confessors of the hope of Israel. This—the resurrection of the dead—was an article in the Pharisee's confession of faith, which Paul had not denied; nay, rather, he had found the kernel of the nut in "the First-Fruits" of the resurrection; in Him Israel's hope had become alive. The chief captain would turn with a contemptuous smile from the disorderly

---

by quotations from Luther, in his comment on the Acts. I certainly think, with the learned author, that the Apostle could not well mistake the high priest; but I take his "I wist not," to mean "I lost sight of,"—"did not bear in mind;" an admission certainly implying a severe reflection; for had Ananias' bearing been in consonance with his office, Paul could not have forgotten himself, *i.e.*, lost sight of his being the high priest. A comparison with other passages justifies this sense of the Greek word; for instance, Eph. vi. 8, and Col. iii. 24, in both which places, the English "knowing" is quite tantamount to "bearing in mind."—Tr.

uproar in the holy Sanhedrim, and fearing for his prisoner, "lest he should have been pulled in pieces of them," he had him brought into the castle, where, lying in darkness, "the Lord stood by" His troubled and comfort-needing servant, saying unto him, "Be of good cheer, Paul: for as thou hast testified of me in Jerusalem, so must thou bear witness also at Rome." This, "thou must," he caught hold of with firm faith, and yet trod the wondrous path traced for him by God, so soberly and circumspectly, that he did not think his young nephew too mean an angel to disappoint those forty Jewish zealots who conspired against his life. He evidently had won upon the Roman captain by his manly and collected bearing, and the whole charm of his character. Yet, without some palpable official cause, his personal favour and sympathy for the prisoner would hardly have induced Claudius Lysias to risk his popularity by summoning military force to his protection. It is, indeed, an edifying spectacle this nightly transport from Jerusalem to Cæsarea. "Who Thee serves, Thou mighty Lord, may bid defiance to the world!" Now Paul is in the hands of governor Felix, a profligate, who, as Tacitus has it, under the guise of cruelty concealed a servile soul. He was to feel the weight of this singular prisoner's testimony, and quail beneath it. (Cf. Acts xxiii.)

Against the accusations of the Jews, who came down to Cæsarea with a hired attorney, the "ringleader of the sect of the Nazarenes," this "pestilent fellow,"—as Tertullus *is* pleased to designate him,—answers with *singular appropriateness*, and with the fearlessness of which he writes, (Rom. xiii. 3,) "Wilt thou not be afraid of the power? do that which is good." Felix was not unacquainted with the Christian way, though his own was the broad one. Therefore the Apostle could expect him to understand, that the Christians were only the legitimate Jews, which was the drift of Paul's defence before him, who was bound by his office to protect that nation in the exercise of their religion. With all the composure and circumspection which the case called for, he omitted not to make a thrust into this new Pilate's conscience, by lighting on it with the testimony of Israel's hope, the resurrection of the dead, "both of the just and unjust." Unscrupulous as he was, yet Felix so far conformed to the duty of his office, that he would not deliver Paul to the Jewish court of justice, but left the case in suspense, meanwhile extending to his prisoner a mild treatment in Herod's court-house. To indulge his amorous wife, Drusilla, "which was a Jewess," with a piquant entertainment on the subject of her religion, he had Paul summoned into their presence. But Paul was no lover of soft raiment. Like John the Baptist, before Herod Antipas, he stood before Felix, and reasoned with him and his Herod's daughter, "of righteousness, temperance, and judgment to come." Whereat the sensual worldling "trembled," and stammered out a civil phrase, to rid himself of the truth by dissembling compliment. By degrees, however, he unlearned this trembling before the bound preacher of the unbound word, and thinking, after the maxim of a true worldling, that even this Nazarene's uprightness must have its price, he put up for two years with his reasonings of temperance, in the hope that "money should have been given him of Paul, that he might loose him." Thus, then, the labourer of the Lord kept involuntary holiday for two years; yet how the dew of heaven descended on him in his lonely cell, we perceive where he comes forth again in the power of God's strength. (Cf. Acts xxiv.)

Felix's successor, Porcius Festus, feels personally greatly inclined " to do the Jews a pleasure," by sacrificing Paul to their bloodthirsty plans, but he *must* protect him. His accusers now proceed to bring a charge of high treason against him. But Paul, not unskilled in law and the rights of a Roman citizen, resists Festus' sinister proposal to send him up for trial to Jerusalem, by appealing to Cæsar; hardly thinking at the time, that what his adversaries now forced him to, would become the very means of fulfilling God's word to him, "Thou must bear witness also at Rome." As yet, however, he had not done with his witness before the unbelieving Jews in Judæa. Herod Agrippa, the son of James' murderer, came down to Cæsarea to greet the new governor; and before this last king of his nation—in a brilliant assembly of polished courtiers, the heads, no doubt, of the civil and military departments at Cæsarea, and all the *élite* of that city—Paul was to close the series of his apostolic defences. (Cf. Acts xxv.)

It is the masterpiece of holy eloquence wherewith the Apostle meets King Agrippa. By his Judaism he seizes this Herod's son, and forces him to bear witness to the unquestionable fact, that conversion to the Lord Jesus is no falling off from the God of Israel, but, contrariwise, the only way for securing the hope of that twelve-tribed nation. After, then, simply stating the ground of a Christian's faith and hope, by narrating his own conversion, in which here he gives prominence to his call as Apostle to the Gentiles, he proceeds to say—" Having, therefore, obtained help of God, I continue unto this day, witnessing both to small and great, saying none other things than those which the prophets and Moses did say should come: that Christ should suffer, and that He should be the first that should rise from the dead, and should shew light unto the people, and to the Gentiles." Here he was interrupted by Festus calling out aloud, "Paul, thou art beside thyself; much learning doth make thee mad." The Roman statesman felt something strangely supernatural in Paul's speech. This prisoner lauds the crucified Jesus as the "light of the Gentiles," and Agrippa listens to him with rapt attention. That would never do, he thought, and deemed it high time to interrupt the enthusiastic speaker. But how must the reply of this madman fall on his astonished ear, when, unoffended, and in complete self-possession—not even omitting his official title, "most noble" Festus—Paul assures him that he speaks the "words of truth and soberness," and appeals to "the king" that these were not matters of fancy, but literal realities; not hidden things done in a corner, but open historical facts. Nor had Paul done with the king yet. A holy fencer, and "not as one that beateth the air," he hits him in the most vulnerable place, in putting, like a flaming sword, the pointed question to him—"King Agrippa, believest thou the prophets?" Embarassing pause! "I know that thou believest," says Paul the prophet; and thus sinks the sword of the Spirit into the heart of a man unable to resist the conviction, that what the prophets have spoken must come to pass. But one step more, and he had believed that it *had* come to pass in Jesus of Nazareth. But this step Bernice's incestuous brother was unwilling to take, and forcing out an easy joke, he replied, "Almost thou persuadest me to be a Christian." But the skilled soldier of Christ knew immediately how to turn to account the beaten king's high-spoken word, by rejoining, in deep earnest, "I would to God that not only thou, but also all that hear me this day, were both almost and altogether such as I am, except these bonds." These, surely, are not the words of a mad enthusiast. His *Christian joy* Paul would have all men to be partakers of; nor did he doubt the Lord's power, who had overcome *him*, to overcome the mightiest, and take the great for a spoil, while his *Christian cross* he would bear, "as of the ability which God giveth," without wishing it upon any other's shoulders. The smile had died on the king's lips, and with hurried despatch he drew to a close the business which had taken so unexpected a turn. He could not help admitting, that the religion of Jesus was unforbidden in the Jewish land. And it is singular enough that, after all, the governor should be compelled to what seemed to him so unreasonable a thing, the sending a prisoner up to Rome, "and not withal signifying the crimes laid against him." (Cf. Acts xxvi.)

The history of his voyage to Italy turns up a new leaf in Paul's life, which we shall find no less edifying to glance over. His serene composure, and yet quick perception, wherewith he knew how to master every situation, we have indeed had repeated occasion already to behold and admire. But here we meet a mutinous crew tamed and led by our captive Jew, who bears a hand himself in the ship as smartly as if he had been a born seaman. Our first look is fixed properly upon the hand of the Lord, who gives as a prize to His servant those very men that carried him captive to Rome; but it affords St Luke an evident pleasure to paint in its minutest details the conduct of his beloved Paul, through whom, as his instrument, the Lord brings about what He pleases to the joy of His Church. The Adramyttian ship from the harbour of Cæsarea, and the Alexandrian which sailed from Myra, bare the precious freight, which was at length to still the longings of the distant "isles," (Isa. xlii. 4, li. 5, lx. 9.) Satan would fain have made the deep, that calls him lord, to become the grave of his stout adversary. But to "perils in the sea" the Apostle was not unused, for thrice he had suffered shipwreck, a night and a day he had been in the deep, (2 Cor. xi. 25.) Nowise doubting the Lord's safe guidance, who had ensured his life by His own words, yet Paul knew that he was not on board as dead cargo, but as a living Christian man; and no sooner did the approaching tempest threaten to endanger their passage in the Mediterranean, than he stepped forward with his counsel, advising them to run in and winter at Crete, in a harbour called "The Fair Havens." "Nevertheless the centurion" of the imperial life-guards at Cæsarea, who had charge of Paul, friendly as he was to him, "believed the master and the owner of the ship," more than the "missionary." However, it went so badly with their discipline on board, that neither master nor owner, who both wished to hasten with corn to the Italian market, could gain their point, for "the more part" preferred to run into another harbour of Crete, which offered them a more agreeable sojourn for wintering. This was confusion worse confounded. Meanwhile, the wind called "Euroclydon" really arose, and no skill of the most skilful could now do aught with the ship; so they "let her drive." Then Paul turned sailor, with both Luke and Aristarchus his companions, and won favour with the crew by "bearing a hand" in getting up the boat, undergirding the ship, and lightening her by heaving her gear overboard. Still all was in vain. Three sunless days and still worse starless nights they were driven to and fro upon the tempest-tossed waves; and "all hope that we should be saved was then taken away," writes Luke. But then was shewn what, under God, one man's word can accomplish. Amid the despairing crowd, staring into their watery grave, which is yawning before them, Paul steps forth, and having reproved their wanton rejection of his counsel, he says, "And now, I exhort you to be of good cheer, for there shall be no loss of any man's life among you, but of the ship." What! is Paul going to bear them all upon his back, and swim with them to the unseen land? No, but upon his heart he has borne them. "*For there stood by me,*" he continues, "*this night the angel of God, whose I am, and whom I serve, saying, Fear not, Paul: thou must be brought before Cæsar; and lo, God hath given thee all them that sail with thee.*" He that can thus depict and magnify the Lord's goodness will also draw Gentile hearts, and find open ears, when he preaches Him to them. Paul has turned "naval chaplain," and the crew have heard a life-sermon. The whole had to acknowledge themselves his prize, not even Julius the centurion excepted. "*Wherefore, sirs,*" he joyfully continues, "*be of good cheer: for I believe God, that it shall be even as He hath told me.*" This is his sheet-anchor—faith, the rope which he throws to the hopeless, that they may cling to it and be safe. But one demand he has to make along with it. They must relinquish all thoughts of saving the ship, and with their bare lives must be stranded on an island. Will they do it? Are they going into the "life-boat" of Paul's word, and abandon the planks they are still treading? Not immediately. They sound first, and find it twenty fathoms, and next fifteen. Then fearing lest they should run upon rocks, they cast four anchors astern, and wish for the day. Now the crew, under colour of casting anchors out of the foreship also, stealthily let the boat down into the sea, in order to make their escape in it at break of day. But Paul, amid the night's confusion, perceived their design, and called out to the centurion and soldiers, "*Except these abide in the ship, ye cannot be saved.*" How differently would the mythic muse equip and deck out her hero! Paul looks upon the prize God hath given him, not as machines, but men, who, with meek submission, have to enter into God's will for their salvation, and to bestir themselves in that way which it shall please God to point out for their rescue. Look, with what elastic buoyancy, and yet iron firmness, this hero of faith puts his whole man in motion; his every sense and reason he places as means at God's disposal, to work His will. With all his perfect self-surrender to God, he never loses self-possession; with all his depth of tender feeling, there is no sentimentality; with all the deep rest of a broken heart, there is no confused mysticism; with all his affections set on the things above—having "tasted the powers of the world to come" —there is no want of sense for this life, nor any monkish depreciation of it; with all the implicit obedience of the bondman of Christ, he yet possesses the firmest energy of will and thorough manliness. For a long time I could not understand why Luke should have sketched the history of this voyage with so lingering a pencil. In my comment on this chapter, I have mainly endeavoured to shew what position Paul's voyage to Italy occupies in the holy drama of "the Acts of the Apostles, or rather the history of the deeds, through them, of the risen and exalted Saviour in His primitive church." But in the epos also of Paul's life, in the picture of his character, the history of this voyage shines forth in the lustre of primeval freshness. Can we still wonder that Paul has won the Roman Julius' heart? Upon his word he orders his soldiers to "cut off the ropes of the boat, and let her fall off." That was strong faith, strengthened by Paul's own. Now every bridge of human help is cut off, and the "life-boat" of Paul's word held firm by the safety-rope of the Almighty's faithfulness— their only refuge. As daylight came on, Paul yet once more stepped forth among the crew, who looked desponding after a fortnight's fast, and winningly beseeching them to take courage, and "to take meat for their health," he adds, "for there shall not an hair fall from the head of any of you." And lo, they hearken to his voice amid the roaring sea, whose every surging billow threatens to snap the fragile cables, and dash the vessel to pieces on the rocks. "And when he had thus spoken, he took bread, and gave thanks to God in presence of them all; and when he had broken it, he began to eat." In truth an heroic meal! and his fervent "grace" in breaking the bread, won upon all the two hundred and seventy-six souls, whom God had given him: "Then were they all of good cheer; and they also took some meat." "And when they had eaten enough, they forthwith cast the wheat into the sea," took up the anchors, loosed the rudder-bands, hoised the mainsail to the wind, and made toward the shore of an unknown isle. Driven betwixt two seas which met, they soon ran aground with such force, that "the forepart of the ship stuck fast, and remained unmoveable, but the hinder part was broken with the violence of the waves." Seeing some bent on their escape by jumping overboard, "the soldiers' counsel was to kill the prisoners." Their duty, truly Roman! stood above their gratitude. But the centurion, "willing to save Paul,"—to the very last it is the arm of a man, directed by God, that shields the Apostle's life—"kept them from their purpose;" and upon his military command, "those that could swim" had to "cast themselves first into the sea," and get to land, in order to draw those ashore that drifted after, on boards and broken pieces of the ship. "And so," by straining every human nerve to the last, "it came to pass, that they escaped all safe to land." Thus the Almighty humbly hid His wondrous help under cover of the human; and Paul has comprehended God's manner, which is not that of pointing a pistol to a man's breast, with a peremptory, "Believe, or die!" (Cf. Acts xxvii.)

It was only after they had reached the island in safety —which proved to be Malta—that the shipwrecked party came to know their deliverer, as one of those who should have "power to tread on serpents and scorpions." Him who had shared all the hardships and necessities of the ship—who had proved himself a naval hero, rather than a churchman—they now saw how he laid hands on the sick of the island, from the house of Publius the chief, to all around that came unto him, and they were healed. After a three months' stay, they departed again, highly honoured, for Paul's sake, and richly furnished with provisions by the hospitable islanders. Under the heathen sign of "Castor and Pollux," the destroyer of heathenism—after spending three days at Syracuse—they safely reached the harbour of Puteoli, where, to their joy, they found "brethren," at whose desire Paul—such was now the centurion's indulgence of his prisoner—was allowed to tarry seven days with them, and thereupon went on to Rome; whence brethren met him, as far as Appii Forum, and the Three Taverns; "whom when Paul saw, he thanked God, and took courage." The sorrow for Jerusalem and Zion's people, which his heart had felt doubly on the voyage that conveyed him from them, had made him no way incapable of acting as we have seen him do. Who of the ship's company would have thought that this heroic prisoner was all the while, internally, bowed down under mental sufferings? Yet Luke, not only his "beloved physician," (Col. iv. 14,) but also his trusty brother, discovers to us, that it was only upon the grateful and encouraging sight of the Roman brethren, (Rom. xv. 23, 24,) that the Apostle's mournful sorrow was changed into joyful thanksgiving. Their fall is the riches of the world, (Rom. xi. 12;) this he now saw with his eyes and took courage—to go on with the graffing in of "the wild olive-tree" among the broken off "natural branches," in order that "the good olive-tree" might bud again and flourish in many Gentile branches; while those "broken off in unbelief" he commended to the

## THE PRISONER OF JESUS CHRIST. 93

goodness of God, "who is able to graff them in again." A prisoner, and yet triumphant, Paul enters Rome. (Cf. Acts xxviii. 1-15.)

Julius the centurion's favourable report to the captain of the imperial guard, procured Paul the liberty of staying where he pleased, with only a soldier for his guard. With unshaken fidelity to his nation, and with inexhaustible patience, also here at Rome, he addressed himself first to his own brethren after the flesh, and sought to gain their confidence. Compelled to claim Cæsar's protection from his Jewish persecutors, yet would he have naught to accuse his nation of, rather declaring, "For the hope of Israel I am bound with this chain." But, alas! he found the Jews the same at Rome as everywhere else, and with Isaiah's woe he is forced to take leave of them. Having tried in vain, "from morning till evening," to "persuade them concerning Jesus, both out of the law of Moses, and out of the prophets," he has recoursé again to what is everywhere his last resource with them, *i.e.*, provoking them to jealousy by the salvation of the Gentiles; and concludes, " Be it known, therefore, unto you, that the salvation of God is sent unto the Gentiles, and that they *will* hear it." And they *have* heard it. Two whole years Paul dwelt at Rome in his own hired house, and received all that came in unto him; preaching in this capital of the world the kingdom of God—in the residence of Cæsar whom the world called "Lord," (Acts xxv. 26,) the name of the Lord Jesus, inwardly with all confidence, outwardly without restraint; an ambassador of Christ, wearing the chain, not indeed of an imperial order, but of an imperial prisoner—in token of the suffering state of Christ's Church. But the Word of God was not bound; that sufficed him. (Cf. Acts xxviii. 16-31.)

That, upon the expiration of these two years, Paul's

long-pending trial does not yet terminate in his execution, some slight hints in the Acts, and more in his Epistles, seem to indicate. The ancient Church, too—already, it should seem, Clemens Romanus, his own disciple—almost uniformly thought, that the Apostle was permitted to accomplish his purposed journey into Spain, (Rom. xv. 24;) and of a return to the East his Second Epistle to Timothy shews evident traces. (Cf. 2 Tim. iv. 13, 20, passages which can hardly suit Paul's first journey from Corinth, *viâ* Jerusalem, to Rome.) Whence this epistle—the Apostle's last legacy to the Church—must have been, and, in fact, was written during a second imprisonment of Paul at Rome, and in view of his near martyrdom, (2 Tim. iv. 6-8,) which, according to the unanimous testimony of the ancients, he suffered by the sword under Nero. But for a sketch of him after the Word of God, Luke has set us the limits. One glance, however, we must still cast upon the letters which the Apostle wrote during his two years' detention at Rome. They are effusions of holy joy from the prisoner of the Lord. That to the Ephesians, a circular epistle to the churches in and about Ephesus, is a "song of degrees," set for the Church of Christ. In it he contemplates with holy ecstasy God's marvel-building reared of living souls, and growing together unto an holy temple in the Lord, as the historical realisation of "the mystery of Christ." Hand in hand with this goes that to the Colossians, which breathes all the heavenly joy of a cross-honoured confessor. With prominent lustre shines in it the word of Christ, as the all-sufficient treasure of His Church. Most earnestly does the Apostle exhort "the saints and faithful brethren in Christ," in firm faith and pure doctrine to "hold the Head, and to cling unwaveringly to Him, in whom dwelleth all the fulness of the Godhead bodily," bewaring of all deceit and beguiling of their reward by any dreamy, self-chosen, or affected spirituality. In his Philippian epistle, Paul's heart leaps for joy, and cannot be sad: a dozen times and more the words "joy" and "rejoice" occur in it. The Philippian Church—this pearl of his first-love (remember Acts xvi.)—remained his jewel through life. He cheerfully accepted their "ministering unto his necessities," and they were also privileged to "communicate with his affliction" even at Rome. "To abide in the flesh," and continue with them for their "furtherance and joy of faith," struggled in him with the desire "to depart and be with Christ," the sole gain of his life, and the fountain of all his joy, whereout to drink righteousness and peace became daily more precious to his soul. With "great joy" also he writes to Philemon. All the grace and loveliness of a manly soul breathes its rich perfume through this little letter of "Paul the aged," who in his bonds plays merrily on words, beseeching Philemon to place to his account, as partner, aught Onesimus, once servant, now a brother, might be indebted to their joint-firm of love. Finally the "Hebrews" saluted by the "Gentile" churches. ("They of Italy salute you," Heb. xiii. 24.) For though we can hardly allow Paul himself to be the author of this epistle, (chap. ii. 3;)—the word of salvation "was confirmed unto us by them that heard him," already forbids this;— yet that the Holy Ghost, as He was in Paul, inspired it, is sure enough, and that Luke is the author commissioned and counselled by the Apostle, we may deem very probable.\* As the Apostle saw the day of "judgment and

\* In this view I cannot concur. Taking the Apostle to speak in the name of the Hebrews, as undoubtedly he does in Heb. ii. 3, (cf. v. 1,) every difficulty (which the author feels) of reconciling this passage with Gal. i. 12, falls of course to the ground; and by "them that heard him" are evidently meant their late teachers, principally James, the Lord's brother, who had "spoken unto them the word of God," (Heb. xiii. 7.) But we certainly have the strongest correlative evidence for Paul, and fiery indignation" impend over Jerusalem, (Heb. x. 25-27,) his affectionate heart was stirred by love to his never forgotten Hebrew brethren, to strengthen their shaken confidence by his testifying—but no, perhaps they would rather hear it from another than himself—by one of his fellow-helpers testifying to them of the immovable kingdom, and its imperishable blessings, as theirs by inheritance; and by magnifying to them the great High Priest of the heavenly sanctuary, before whose glory the splendour of Zion's superannuated tabernacle fades.

Through the whole way, in which we have followed the track of Paul's feet, we have seen fulfilled to himself the prayer he offers up with bended knees for the Ephesians, that the Father of our Lord Jesus Christ would grant them, according to the riches of His glory, to be strengthened with might by His Spirit in the inner man, (Eph. iii. 16.) In acting, in speaking and writing, in suffering and in silent rest, all is of one cast throughout—he is as much "every inch a Christian," as he is "every inch a man;" the crown of his heroic character being the offering up of himself to "please Him who hath chosen him to be a soldier," (2 Tim. ii. 4.) "Christ is all and in all," (Col. iii. 11,) was his symbolum. To live unto Christ in all things was his glory, and to "present every man perfect in Christ Jesus," the aim of all his life. Does the greatness of this man oppress thee, instead of elevating thee? Behold, "by the grace of God I am what I am;" and in exhorting his beloved Philippians, "Brethren, be followers together of me, and mark them which walk so as ye have us for an ensample," (Phil. iii. 17;) he expects nothing of his brethren that is beyond the power of the riches of God's grace

---

none other, being the author, in the two passages, Heb. x. 34, and xiii. 18, 19. They are, in fact, hardly short of conclusive proof, on which his authorship may securely rest.—TR.

working in them both to will and to do, (Phil. ii. 13.) It shall be done, if we will but tread in the blessed footsteps of Paul's faith.

> "Wouldst thou inherit life with Christ on high?
> Then count the cost, and know,
> That here on earth below
> Thou needs must suffer with the Lord and die.
> We reach the gain, to which all else is loss
> But through the Cross."

## VII.

## THE MAN OF FAITH.

"We having the same spirit of faith, according as it is written, I believed, and therefore have I spoken; we also believe, and therefore speak."
—2 Cor. iv. 13.

A MAN Paul was, in the full sense of the word. To what glory (2 Cor. iii. 18) fallen man, created after God's image, may be renewed, is seen in Paul, as hardly in any other. Is spiritual life ruled by the holy triumvirate of these three, —faith, hope, charity? (1 Cor. xiii. 13.) Then Paul became the man he was by the harmonious reign in him of these three fundamental graces. An enemy to all half-heartedness, ever thoroughly decided for what attracted his soul, he apprehended Jesus by *faith* the moment he was apprehended of Him by grace, and at once renounced all he had counted gain after the flesh without Christ; and then, in pressing toward the mark for the prize of his high calling, he forgets all that is behind, reaching forth in living *hope* unto those things which are before, and has already his "conversation in heaven, from whence also we look for the Saviour, the Lord Jesus Christ;" and unto Him he lived with that devoted *love*, wherein the Christian's future heavenly likeness of Christ has its present beginning on earth; and he was a man also in love, heroically sacrificing himself for the good of his brethren.—Faith, hope, love, these three, in their threefold oneness, stood continually before the eyes of his mind, (Eph. i. 15, 18; Phil. i. 9, &c.;

Col. i. 4, 23; 1 Thess. i. 3, v. 8; 2 Thess. i. 3; Tit. i. 1, &c.; Heb. vi. 10, &c., x. 22-24.) But to see the charm of them in their combined loveliness, read the whole of his Epistle to the Philippians.

We may doubtless reckon upon universal consent in designating Paul as "the man of faith." But against the merit some attach to him, when they extol his faith, Paul, "the servant of Jesus Christ," protests with all his might. They vainly imagine a Paul that will patronise their "liberty of conscience," and the acting "in good faith" according to their conviction; and they absolutely will not see that as regards the much-loved liberty, according to which every one is to be saved "after his own fashion," it haply might be sought with heathen Gallio, but is utterly rejected by the minister and confessor of Jesus Christ. He only prizes—but that highly—man's liberation from the bondage of sin unto "obedience to the faith," (Acts vi. 7; Rom. i. 5, xvi. 26;) and this obedience to the faith he prizes not as a human virtue, but as the result of the gracious power of God through "the gospel of Christ," (Rom. i. 16.) Faith, in Paul's sense of it, is the Christ-betrothed soul's weddingring, the preciousness of which lies not in the holding of it, but in Him that is held by it—viz., in Jesus Christ. "But we have this treasure in earthen vessels," not in mortal only, but also sinful, bodies, in which flesh and spirit are at continual war, "that the excellency of the power may be of God, and not of us," (2 Cor. iv. 7.) If ever a Christian man could have been tempted to rejoice in his devotion to Christ, as an heroic deed, which might avail aught before God, and deserve His praise, it must have been Paul; but he allowed the truth of this word to illumine his path. The promise therefore is of faith, that it might be by grace; to the end it might be sure, (Rom. iv. 16.) To be saved of God by grace, not on account of faith, but through faith, for Christ's sake, is his unvaried creed. We admire the heroic strength of his faith, after the manner of Abraham's, (Rom. iv. 18, &c.,) but nowise find in it any meritorious cause of his salvation. Otherwise it had been the man Paul who saved himself by virtue of his faith. Let it rather rest thus: Paul's manliness in faith shews itself in his energetic passiveness to the active grace of God in Christ—operating upon and in him. So then, "all praise is ever God's, while ours is the joy."

We now resume the thread at the great turning-point of Paul's life, where, in his conversion by the heavenly call, which made him the won of the Lord Jesus, we beheld the first unfolding of the productive seed of Divine grace,—an unfolding which stands complete before us in the Apostle's evangelical preaching. That Paul *so* preached and wrote, as needs he must, to make his word *apostolic*, the norm and rule of Christian doctrine,—thereunto he was inspired by the Spirit of God; and he was in solemn earnest, when he said, "Which things also we speak, not in the words which man's wisdom teacheth, but which the Holy Ghost teacheth," (1 Cor. ii. 13.) Yet did he not speak like a tinkling cymbal giving forth the sound made on it by another, but like a living Christian, whose whole man—body, soul, and spirit—is constantly under the operation of Divine grace by the Spirit of *faith*. And thus, without prejudice to the doctrine of Inspiration, we abide by this, that the Gospel Paul preaches is the testimony of his own experience. He has seen the crucified and risen Jesus, and He has been revealed to him as the Christ, the Son of God. In Him, through faith in His name, he has received—by the mouth of Ananias, and under his baptizing hand—the forgiveness of his sins, salvation, and life. Jesus Christ, therefore, is the sum and substance both of his own faith and of the faith which he preaches. Nothing he determined to know save Jesus Christ and Him crucified, (1 Cor. ii. 2,) true to the maxim: "Preach one thing, and one thing only—the wisdom of the Cross!" When, therefore, he desires to sum up shortly and well the faith he preaches, he does it in this manner: "If thou shalt confess with thy mouth the Lord Jesus, and shalt believe in thine heart that God hath raised Him from the dead, thou shalt be saved," (Rom. x. 9.)

The first knowledge Paul gained from this wisdom of the cross was, that he felt himself a lost and condemned sinner, who in no other way can possibly be saved than simply in that of faith in Christ. For in the light that issues from the Cross,—that is, from Him that hangs upon it, who is both David's Son and Son of God,—he beholds the enmity slain, even the law of commandments, and peace made through the blood of His cross, (Eph. ii. 14-16; Col. i. 20.) The bitterest enmity of the carnal mind against God, (Rom. viii. 7,) centred in that of the Jews against His Christ. "When Jesus therefore had taken the vinegar, He said, It is finished," (John xix. 31.) The sin of His people, the sin of mankind here exhausted itself upon Him. He clean drank it out of the sponge of vinegar by His saving thirst; and God's wrath against sinners, by reason of His holiness, is clean done away, and peace made, through the reconciling blood of Jesus Christ, (Rom. v. 9, 10; Col. i. 20-22;) who has felt and borne to the utmost, even to the bitter point of being forsaken of God, the curse of God's wrath upon sin; thus doing away—for all that believe in Him—the punishment of sin by bearing it Himself. This is God's atoning mercy through Christ, Paul's glory of faith in Christ, (Rom. v. 11; 2 Cor. v. 19-21.) Because he had been chief among the persecutors of Jesus, filling the vinegared sponge with the bitterness of his enmity, therefore he counted himself the chief of sinners; but therefore also he adored the exceeding love of God in Christ, with the overpowering thankfulness of a child of grace: " But God, who is rich in mercy, for His great love wherewith He loved us, even when we were dead in sins, hath quickened us together with Christ; (by grace ye are saved;) and hath raised us up together, and made us sit together in heavenly places in Christ Jesus; that in the ages to come He might shew the exceeding riches of His grace, in His kindness toward us through Christ Jesus. For by grace are ye saved through faith; and that not of yourselves: it is the gift of God: not of works, lest any man should boast," (Eph. ii. 4-9.)

"Dead in sins," so the Apostle expresses man's condition without Christ; not sick only, but dead; not partially corrupt, but dead. His doctrine of man's corruption through sin is that of a man who had thoroughly experienced that through Adam's fall man's nature has become so wholly corrupt, that "there is no health in us:" though himself had never wallowed in the mire of sin, but rather had from a child looked with detestation upon all heathen abominations. But the nobler, according to human reason, his moral aspirations had been, the more determinedly he had exerted all the strength of his natural will to attain unto the righteousness required by the law,—the more penetrated he was now with the conviction, that "by the works of the law no flesh shall be justified before God," (Rom. iii. 20; Gal. ii. 16.) His own bitter experience, which had abundantly proved what carnal Judaism, carried to the utmost stretch, was able to effect, emboldened him to the assertion, that by the law *every mouth* is stopped, and *all the world* becomes guilty before God, (Rom. iii. 19.) By manifesting the law to Israel, God lighted up the dying embers of legal light still glimmering in the human heart, (Rom. ii. 15,) and convinced all mankind that the law's

"Thou shalt," and "Thou shalt not," are unable to help man unto life by righteousness. For in the midst of Israel sin abounded to the very killing of God's own Son, and it was so to abound, (Rom. v. 20,) that a despairing Saul might fall into the arms of still more abounding grace, and hence preach to a guilty world the redemption we have in Christ's blood. God's light having shined into his own Pharisaic darkness, (2 Cor. iv. 6,) Paul's righteousness by faith shines bright everywhere in the light of its antithesis to that by the law. The benefit of this lies in its pedagogic discipline, which he, the true Israelite, concedes to all nations. Two fundamental tones betoken the voice of this—if we may so say—Universal Apostle. The one is—There is no difference between Jews and Gentiles, as regards their bondage under sin, (Rom. iii. 9,) in which all have been dead, and are therefore all alike—Jews as Gentiles—"by nature the children of wrath," (Eph. ii. 1–3;) and the other is—There is no difference between Jews and Gentiles in their obtaining God's grace, (Rom. x. 12;) for all that are partakers of Abraham's faith are the children of promise, and are made righteous and heirs of eternal life, solely through faith in Jesus Christ, (Rom. iv. 11; Gal. iii. 28.) As all the world is guilty before God, so it is also reconciled unto Him; for "God was in Christ reconciling the world unto Himself," (2 Cor. v. 19.) The priestly-central position of Israel for all tribes on earth had been the highest pride of youthful Saul; but it was only when the scales fell from his Pharisaic eyes that Paul understood Israel's glory: Christ, who is over all, God blessed for ever, as concerning the flesh, cometh of Israel, (Rom. ix. 5;) being found in fashion as a man, He humbled Himself, and was made under the law, (Phil. ii. 8; Gal. iv. 4;) that the blessing of Abraham might come on the Gentiles through Jesus Christ, (Gal. iii. 14.) Instead of law's partition-wall between Jew and Gentile, which He broke down, He now reared Israel's enlarged gospel-tent, lengthening her cords and strengthening her stakes all over the earth, Himself standing between God and all mankind, the all-sufficient propitiation through faith in His blood, (Rom. iii. 25.) Or "is he the God of the Jews only?" Paul asks his Hebrew brethren, "Is he not also of the Gentiles? Yes, of the Gentiles also," (Rom. iii. 29.) Through One upon all — this is the Apostle's spirited and cogent argument in the fifth of Romans. His faith was truly catholic: All-prevailing sin, all-prevailing grace; all-reigning death, all-reigning life; all-crushing condemnation, all-establishing justification. This was the fountain whence he drew his strength. "I believe, and therefore do I speak." He believed with all his heart that Christ's word, "It is finished," dropped peace on all mankind. As of one blood—Adam's—he saw all nations of men to dwell on the face of the earth; so through one blood—Christ's—he saw all mankind reconciled. Of the loss of all in Adam he was sure, but—thanks be to God!—as sure of the gain of all in Christ, the Chief and Leader of a new mankind. "For as in Adam all die, even so in Christ shall all be made alive," (1 Cor. xv. 22.)

All that are in Christ by faith. Paul must have robbed the inmost sanctuary of his Christian heart, had he supposed Faith to be a deed, or even the joint-deed, of man's "free will." The man lying in the dust before the gates of Damascus would have given him the lie. To say that God's grace draws that in man, which is akin to Him, and that He rewards man's good-will in proportion to its yielding to such drawing, is a fable told to whitewash nature. Paul knows nothing of it; but only of undeserved mercy shewn to him, that is, of such mercy that has no ground save in itself. We feel how he gives his own flesh a death-blow every time that he strips man of all claim to self-esteem and merit before God. By faith in Christ he understood the history of man's redemption, from first to last, to be one of supremely free grace. Sure as he was that, while in unbelief, though of Israel, he was not heir to Israel's promise; so sure he was also that the promises of God's word to the true Israel remained steadfast, in spite of the whole mass of unbelief in Israel after the flesh. He calls prophets and patriarchs to witness the ever and anon manifested principle of salvation, according to which those are saved in whose hearts the grace of the Caller effects the purpose of the Chooser to the obtaining of mercy by receiving Faith. "I will have mercy on whom I will have mercy, and I will have compassion on whom I will have compassion." This word spoken to Moses is precious to Paul; for it shews Him who is "gracious and merciful" to be Himself the sole cause of His grace and mercy, to the exclusion of all and every merit of man's co-operation. Yea, the Apostle boldly proceeds to the very sharpest point of Scripture-proof: "Therefore hath He mercy on whom He will have mercy, and whom He will He hardeneth;" and shews by the example of Pharaoh, that even the unbeliever's wicked will is powerless against God; but being hardened by resisting God's good-will, is brought to serve the irresistible will of his Maker. How much more, then, will God's gracious and merciful will save believers, independent of all preventive doing on the part of man, yea, unmixed with any self-acting of the human will! "So then it is not of him that willeth, nor of him that runneth, but of God that sheweth mercy." Fearless of man's reasoning: "Why doth He yet find fault; for who hath resisted His will?" the Apostle reposes with all believers in the bosom of the Triune-God's eternal "love," "wherewith," foreknowing, forechoosing, and foreordaining, "He hath loved" Abraham's race in Abraham's seed, and Adam's race in the second Adam,—the Son of man,—who hath given Himself to become the Author of man's salvation. In Him,—the Lord Jesus,—as in the open book of life, Paul read his own and his brethren's names, (Phil. iv. 3,) written before the foundation of the world, (Eph. i. 4;) and to be chosen in Him the Beloved, according to God's eternal purpose of love—this was the firm rock of his faith, which no deluge could shake, (Rom. viii. 28, &c.) But could an objection like the following escape the thinking Paul? If salvation is not of him that willeth, nor of him that runneth, but of God that sheweth mercy, there can be but these two alternatives: Either God will have mercy on all, and work in their hearts faith to receive His grace; and then all men must finally be saved, by reason of His irresistible will; or God will have mercy only on some, on others not; works therefore faith in some, and hardens others in unbelief, according to the absolute will of His choice; and then Christ is not the Mediator and Redeemer of all; and God is not all light and love, but there is darkness and unlove in Him? Surely Paul needed no one to usher up such syllogisms to his mind, as he wrote Rom. ix. But bold and fearless as he is in pondering over the revealed ways and judgments of God, he is no less so in subduing, yea, in crushing his own reason, where it seeks to darken and unsettle Christ,—God in Christ,—as revealed to us in His Word and work. Predestination to him is a Divine mystery full of comfort and assurance to faith. But both the system of the would-be wise, who desire to make God the slave of His own decrees, and degrade man to a machine in the world's great workshop, and the sinister artfulness of the work-proud, who, by their "necessary consequences" from it, seek to lead that apostolic doctrine to an absurd result, Paul, the man of faith, crushes in one blow, by saying, "We bring into captivity every thought to the obedience of Christ," (2 Cor. x. 5.) He can bear not to know the solution of these mysteries; in man the ability not to will, with the inability to will; and in God the will that all men shall be saved, with the will that "he that believeth not shall be damned." He can rejoice and praise God, who in mercy hath fastened in his life "a nail in a sure place," to which he knows himself securely fixed, according to God's eternal purpose of his choice in Christ; and he checks every forward thought of a twofold, coeternal purpose in God foredetermining the lot of each individual, either to the right hand or left. Instead of speculating, he adores, (Rom. xi. 33-36.)

Paul knows the All-merciful to be the righteous Judge, (2 Tim. iv. 8.) Drawn before His judgment-seat, and witnessed against by His accusing law, he has heard the sentence, "Thou art guilty of death;" but he has also seen the Surety, "who has blotted out the handwriting against him, and nailed it to the cross," (Col. ii. 14.) With him justification and the forgiveness of sin are essentially one, (Rom. iv. 6-8,) and mercy's full reprieve is sure to him, because it is the righteous Judge, who pronounces the sentence of grace. "We are," he writes in that cardinal passage of the Romans, "justified freely by His grace, through the redemption that is in Christ Jesus; whom God hath set forth to be a propitiation through faith in His blood, to declare His righteousness for the remission of sins that are past; to declare, I say, at this time His righteousness; that He might be just, and the justifier of him which believeth in Jesus," (Rom. iii. 24-26.) "Sin could not unrevenged remain, Its sentence had been long declared, And executed it must one day be Here on this wicked earth. What sin was, and what long it had deserved, God would bear witness; and in man's redemption He broke His silence, shewing wrath severe." These lines of Freylinghausen exactly hit Paul's meaning. That our God is a consuming fire, (Heb. xii. 29,) was by no means stripped off his creed, as an antiquated Jewish notion, but was only rightly understood by him in the light of Christ's cross. Therefore he has nothing to do with the effeminate or light-minded, who fancy themselves free from God's wrath, and call the dreams of their imagination faith. The rock, whereon his faith was founded, is Christ and His blood;. and the righteousness by faith, wherein he boldly appeared before God, is purely and entirely a gift of grace (Rom. v. 17) purchased by Christ's obedience and satisfaction. Here, in the matter of justification, he has learnt what faith is—viz., the heart's mouth opened by Divine grace to receive into it Jesus Christ, and all the treasures of His merits purchased for us by His blood. Imputed, and therefore complete, is the righteousness faith has in Him, (Rom. iv. 3, &c.; Phil. iii. 9.) Not unto us, but unto Christ in our stead, hath God imputed our sins, (2 Cor. v. 19-21,) and hath condemned sin in the flesh of His own Son, (Rom. viii. 3,) in order that both righteously and graciously He might, by a gospel-declaration, impute us Christ's righteousness. Luther's precious word "alone" in Rom. iii. 28, though it does not stand there in Greek letters, yet stands clear and bright in Paul's heart: *By faith alone.* All works of the law, be they "preventing" or "accompanying;" yea, and all of the soul's renewed will, be they "co-operating" or "following,"—in short, all works Paul will have utterly excluded from the gracious act of the sinner's justification. The "gift of righteousness" is to be by faith alone. Each and every addition of work to faith is a poison to faith. Grace the giver, faith the receiver: this is Paul's mind and doctrine. Grace will reign *supreme*, or not at all; will be received by faith alone, or remain at a distance. The light of the Sun of Grace is so delicate, so pure and transparent, that it can bear no mixture with the slightest glare of a strange fire; yea, the reflection even of her own brightness ("faith of itself gives forth the shine,") she will not bear being mixed with herself, where the shadeless brightness and spotless purity is concerned, in which the sinner is to stand righteous before God, (Rom. xi. 6.)

"The prison we were sitting in, gnawing our hearts with sorrow clean, is burst in twain, and we are free!" (cf. Ps. cxxiv. 7.) Such rejoicing of grace's freed children Paul taught us, when by faith he had broken through the prison of sin and the law into the open liberty of the Gospel. Very aptly does the church, on "Lætare" Sunday, read the word: "So then, brethren, we are not children of the bondwoman, but of the free," (Gal. iv. 31.) St Paul is inexhaustible in his praise of the liberty of the righteous by faith, the substance of which he pronounces to be—freedom from the law. And a dearly-purchased freedom this is. For to be freed from its durance by Divine right, we had to get our divorce from it by death; and this has been accomplished in a twofold way: The husband *to whom* we were bound, even the law, was killed when *its* condemnatory sting was broken in the broken body *of* the flesh of our blessed Saviour, and by reason of this we also, who are of the faith of Jesus, have become dead unto the law, to live unto another—viz., to Him who is raised from the dead, (Rom. vii. 1, &c.; 2 Cor. v. 14, 15.) "Through the law I am dead to the law"—thus rejoices the living Paul, (Gal. ii. 19.) As "crucified with Christ" he is dead *through* the law, because the law's curse has been borne and discharged by Him, who "hanged on a tree," (Gal. iii. 13;) and dead *to* the law, because its condemnation having been exhausted upon Christ, those who are baptized into His death are thereby freed from the law, and live by faith in Christ, and unto Him, (Rom. vi. 3-11.) "The law is not made for a righteous man," (1 Tim. i. 9.) But Paul's liberty from "the yoke of bondage," (Gal. v. 1,) is not all told by saying that it is the freedom from law's curse and constraint. It is both this; for from its curse we are redeemed by Christ's all-sufficient satisfaction for us, and from its constraint we are delivered by Christ's Spirit in us, who frees our will, and causes us to "delight in the law of God after the inward man." But it is more still. We are freed also from "the law of commandments contained in ordinances," (Eph. ii. 15.) Through its being inscribed by the Spirit into the hearts of believers, they obey God, not by constraint of the obligatory letter, but by that of the spirit of liberty, (2 Cor. iii. 17,) as His children, (Gal. iv. 5, 6.) In striking contrast with the "spirit of bondage," Paul views the "Spirit of adoption," (Rom. viii. 15.) Now we shall understand the holy wrath, wherewith this manly Paul faces the false brethren, who want to bring again under the yoke of bondage the freemen of Jesus Christ, (Gal. ii. 4, 5.) The truth of the Gospel remains with them only, who through faith "stand fast in the liberty wherewith Christ hath made us free."

"What then? shall we sin, because we are not under the law, but under grace?" (Rom. vi. 15.) Right well did Paul know this question. His old man—Saul the Pharisee—must doubtless often have stoutly equipped himself with it against the doctrine of the Nazarene. But what Paul's graceful disciple, Augustine, thus expresses: "Servitium Domini summa libertas,"—the Lord's service is the highest liberty,—is spoken after the very heart of his great teacher. Emphatically the Apostle calls himself the servant of Jesus Christ; and the servants of righteousness are those over whom sin can reign no more, because they are not under the law, but under grace. The being kept under the law, (Gal. iii. 23,) certainly leads to the knowledge of sin, yea, and to the ever-increasing strength of its hard-felt sway, but never to a breach with it and its power. Terribly kill the law can, but never raise the dead to life. It can pour into the heart of man neither the love of good it commands, nor the hate to evil it enjoins. But what the *Law* cannot do *Grace* can do. With an indignant "God forbid!" Paul scorns away the question, "Shall we sin?" and shews to his brethren how faith makes God's children to be the servants of righteousness unto holiness. Right solidly he speaks in calling all that are freed from the law of sin the bondsmen of righteousness. And as to faith alone he attributes the grace of justification, so also with equal decidedness does he ascribe to it the works of true righteousness in the spiritual life of those that are justified by it. "Yea, we establish the law," (Rom. iii. 31,) says the preacher of faith. It could not establish itself, but it is established through faith—in those that walk after the rule: "We *will* fear and *love* God, that we may keep His commandments;" in the servants of righteousness—who experience Christ to be the end of the law also in this sense, "that the righteousness of the law might be fulfilled in us, who walk not after the flesh, but after the Spirit," (Rom. viii. 4.) Paul's own life is the best refutation of the foolish assertion, that his doctrine tends to Antinomianism. Behold! what a life was that of which he says: "I live, yet not I, but Christ liveth in me: and the life which I now live in the flesh I live by the faith of the Son of God, who loved me, and gave Himself for me," (Gal. ii. 20.) "Brethren, be followers together of me;" thus he dared to exhort his Philippians, (Phil. iii. 17,) whom he wished to be "filled with the fruits of righteousness, which are by Jesus Christ unto the glory and praise of God," (Phil. i. 11.)

And whereby does grace accomplish the work, which in Paul stands so prominently before our eyes? Whereby did this Apostle of Jesus Christ bring to the congregation of saints world-intoxicated Corinthians, Satan-bound Ephesians, and frivolous Romans? As he had himself received salvation, so he communicated it. Not all indeed are apostles, therefore he refers no one to revelations direct from heaven; but all are sinners, like him, and redeemed like him, and in the same way in which he himself became partaker of Christ—viz., by the preaching of the Word and administering of the Sacrament all shall be saved through faith. " Faith cometh by hearing, and hearing by the word of God," (Rom. x. 17.) The word of God is pervaded by the Spirit of God, and filled with "the power of God unto salvation;" whether through oral preaching it first reach the comprehending sense, or first seize by sacramental sign the bodily senses—that the voice, this the kiss, so to speak, of the Spirit. Everywhere the Apostle fastens the Christian's consolation of faith and vigour of life to the creating and preserving word of God's Spirit, which both audibly and visibly, in voice and sacrament, is dispensed in the Church of Christ. Reconciliation, word of reconciliation and ministry of reconciliation, (2 Cor. v. 18, &c.;) faith and baptism, (Eph. iv. 5; Gal. iii. 26, 27;) washing of regeneration and renewing of the Holy Ghost, (Tit. iii. 5;) the hearing of faith and receiving of the Spirit, (Gal. iii. 2;) all these he joins intimately together, and in that beautiful passage, where he makes the faith of righteousness speak Moses' words, which in her mouth become evangelical, he especially adores Christ's reachable nearness to faith, as being present in the Word, (Rom. x. 6, &c.) God the Holy Ghost he sees personally at work in sanctifying believers, (2 Cor. iii. 17, 18,) and to His witness he ascribes the assurance of our adoption as God's children, (Rom. viii. 16.) But not from the store of his "Christian consciousness," or such like subjectivities, did Paul take the witness of the Holy Ghost, but from the Gospel spoken through the ear into his heart, in the name of Jesus: "Thy sins are forgiven thee." This absolution came to him, and comes to all that are baptized into Christ's death (Rom. vi. 3, &c.) through the service of the Church, to which the exalted Christ in heaven has committed the means of grace, and the office, by preaching and administering of the sacraments, to communicate the Holy Ghost,\* "who daily and richly forgiveth mine and all believers' sins; and, by this very forgiveness, beareth witness with my spirit that I am God's child and heir." Do I receive such witness by faith? I am "sealed," (Eph. i. 13;) or, as Luther says, "my experience agreeth with the preached word." Paul lived after the order given by the Lord to him,—"Arise, and go into the city, and it shall be told thee what thou must do," (Acts ix. 6,)—and has taught all men there to look for the grace of Jesus Christ, where He has put the memorial of His name; as it is written, "How beautiful are the feet of them that preach the Gospel of peace, and bring glad tidings of good things," (Rom. x. 15.)

Paul's faith is grounded on God's Word: "So then faith cometh by hearing, and hearing by the word of God," (Rom. x. 17.) The Word of God which he had heard in the Lord's voice from heaven, and through the witness of His Church on earth, he found again in the voice and testimony

---

\* I trust it will meet the author's sense, if we modify this expression by saying, "The Holy Ghost is pleased to communicate *Himself* (ordinarily) through these means;" for so we find it *ever* where the *apostles themselves* were the dispensers of them, (Acts x. 4, xix. 6.) *Only Christ* could say, "Receive ye the Holy Ghost," and "Thy sins be forgiven thee."—TR.

of the same Spirit in Scripture; and richly did his preaching, as his hearing, come by the Word of God. Because he knew and understood the Church of Christ to be the unveiled Israel, the Church's King and Head to be the promised son of David, and the crucified and risen Redeemer to be the real mercy-seat and true Paschal Lamb; therefore he could testify before Agrippa that he "witnessed to both small and great, saying none other things than those which the prophets and Moses did say should come," (Acts xxvi. 22.) "According to the Scriptures"—herewith he seals his delivery of the heaven-received Gospel, (1 Cor. xv. 3, &c.) Who knows not that Paul, in searching the Scriptures, is a very pearl-fisher, a true digger after hidden treasures? He found, and he has delivered to us, the key to all the Scriptures. Luther draws attention to the fact, that in the very Epistle (that to the Romans) which is addressed to a congregation gathered mainly from the Gentiles, the prophetic word, from beginning to end, runs provingly parallel to the apostolic: "Therefore it seemeth as if St Paul in this epistle had wanted for once to compose a manual of the whole Christian and evangelic doctrine, and an introduction into the whole Old Testament. For doubtless he who hath this epistle well in his heart, hath in it also the light and power of the Old Testament." The theme and main topic of this epistle he confirms with Habakkuk's prophecy, "The just shall live by faith," (Rev. i. 17,) from which he unfolds all the Gospel's richest treasures. By Abraham's example he illustrates the righteousness of faith as given by imputation, (Rom. iv.;) and the sacred window in the evangelical edifice, through which we look into the mystery of predestination, he frames round about with the prophetic word, (Rom. ix.-xi.;) nor when treating of the "new commandment" of love does he think that he can do it better, or speak of it more according to the Spirit, than by adducing a prophetic word, (Rom. xii. 19, 20.) He puts Christ before us, as our example in patience, by quoting a word from the Psalms, (Ps. lxix. 9; Rom. xv. 3,) and then adds, (ver. 4,) "For whatsoever things were written aforetime were written for our learning; that we, through patience and comfort of the Scriptures, might have hope." Yea, truly saturated with " comfort of the Scriptures" is his faith; for so he understood them—after the veil was taken from his eyes—that their end and fulfilment is Jesus Christ. Does he view in the light of Holy Writ God's judgments and way of salvation, past, present, and future? (as in Acts xiii., and 1 Cor. x.;) or gather God's accusations against sinners from the law and its expounders, the prophets? (as in Rom. iii.;) or bind bundles of evangelical comfort out of several prophetic passages together? (as in Rom. xi. 26, &c.; and 1 Cor. xv. 54, 55; and especially 2 Cor. vi. 16-18.) Always we see him regard Scripture with reverence, as a sacred whole that cannot be broken, (John x. 35,) and seize it as the sword of the Spirit, (Eph. vi. 17.) " And he doth so," says Luther, " after the manner of his own rich spirit, by smelting a number of passages in one heap, and moulding a text from it, such as bears the sense of the whole Scripture." The "perpetual statute"\* of every word that ever proceeded from the mouth of God he found laid up in store—that is to say, raised and promoted from prediction to fulfilment, unclad of its earthly tabernacle, advanced to heavenly substance, (Heb. viii. 5,) securely *preserved in Christ*. Thus the Apostle of the Gentiles put *them in possession* of Israel's advantage in possessing "the oracles of

---

\* A rather abstruse sentence this. I should think the author must mean that the Apostle looked upon every word of God, though *apparently* but applying to a gone-by or going-by time, as abiding the same for ever, while undergoing the different phases from prediction to fulfilment, from shadow to substance; all being fulfilled and come to substance in Christ.—Tr.

God,"* (Rom. iii. 1, 2.) To the unbelieving Jews the Bible has become a sealed book, (Acts xiii. 27.) In Christ it is opened, and speaks in His Church. "God speaketh in His sanctuary, thereof I am glad," (Ps. cviii. 7, Luther's transl.) The Scripture "saith." And the disciples of the apostolic word gladly sit down with Timothy at the feet of Moses and the prophets, in order to test the truth of Paul's boast of the Scriptures, "Continue thou in the things which thou hast learned, and hast been assured of, knowing of whom thou hast learned them; and that from a child thou hast known the holy Scriptures, which are able to make thee wise unto salvation, through faith which is in Christ Jesus. All Scripture is given by inspiration of God, and is profitable for doctrine, for reproof, for correction, for instruction in righteousness; that the man of God may be perfect, throughly furnished unto all good works," (2 Tim. iii. 14-17.)

But it is in the centre of his Epistle to the Romans that we see to perfection the picture of "the man of faith," in his lament in the 7th and in his triumph in the 8th chapter. Dead to sin, freed from the law, a servant to righteousness, devoted to God's service in newness of the Spirit, made alive from the dead—does all this mean that the renewed Christian is sinless, no more carnal, but completely spiritual, affected by the law no more than the angels that do God's will in heaven, and touched by death no more than the spirits of the just made perfect, who have done with death and all below? Ah! did it mean this, and had

---

* As Jewish scribe already Saul had become familiar with the Hebrew original of the Old Testament. Yet St Paul generally makes use of the official Greek translation, (Septuagint,) because it suited the Gentiles, and had recourse to the Hebrew text only where it was needful or useful. The wisdom of a father, not the interest of a scholastic, guided the interpreter of Scripture.

Paul deemed himself such a saint, then he were not the man of faith he is, and his picture were frightful like a spectre. But our evangelical Saint is comforting and edifying to behold by his fellow-sinners and fellow-saints, to whom there is no condemnation, because they are in Christ Jesus by faith.

He that exhorts his brethren to follow him in the way of holiness would not have them ignorant that faith in the forgiveness of sin was, and ever would be, his sole comfort, not only in regard to his past life without Christ, but also in his present with and in Him. He had put on the Lord Jesus Christ; and being sanctified by the gracious act of justification and regeneration, he was "led of the Spirit," and no longer "under the law," (Gal. v. 18.) Having become conformable and, as it were, akin to the law of the Spirit, he now found in himself, what in his unregenerate state he had never found, that he had a "delight in the law of God after the inward man," and could now look upon it with a clear, unevil eye. That "the statutes of the Lord are right" he had learnt from his youth, but that "they convert the soul and rejoice the heart," (Ps. xix. 7, 8,) he only learnt to know in Christ; and therefore felt constrained to defend the law, as holy, just, and good, against the misconception of his evangelical doctrine and teaching, as though the law were the cause of man's corruption, which it only brings to light. Yet he would have spoken untruth, if by the expressions "it slew me," "and I died," he had meant to represent the deadly effects of the law, as once for all completed in his past experience. Therewith he would have shut himself out from the experience of all his brethren, who, though become dead to both, still feel the law, as still they feel sin, and cry "Woe!" under it. But, on the contrary, he says, " We know that the law is spiritual, but I am carnal, sold under sin." For this *"but I"* we will kiss Paul's hand. The same trials and temptations, against which other Christian men lie in the field,—"I 'gainst myself in deadly combat lie,"—passed over this greatly honoured servant of Christ. He whose faith we desire to follow strengthens our soul by the spiritual gift of his open confession, that as renewed Christian the conflict between flesh and spirit was still his daily experience. The smart of the killing letter therefore was not obsolete, and the use of the law, as working knowledge of sin, no antiquated thing with him. The preacher of liberty from the law never was, nor could be, an Antinomian, because he was *far* from the anti-scriptural notion of having no more sin. What in Gal. v. 17 he thus expresses, "The flesh lusteth against the spirit, and the spirit against the flesh; and these are contrary the one to the other, so that ye cannot do the things that ye would," is the same confession he makes in Rom. vii. Only by daily conflict did he pass to daily victory; and his sigh under the deep smart of sin and death—"Oh, wretched man that I am! who shall deliver me from the body of this death?"—was as much the expression of his present experience, as the triumph of faith by which it is followed, "I thank God through Jesus Christ our Lord." To his great comfort he knew that it was the Lord Jesus who would judge him, (1 Cor. iv. 3-5;) for even where *he* might be unconscious of wrong, ("I know nothing by myself,") he could not deem himself justified, because he had to distrust the sentence of his own conscience, as biased by the flesh. Yet not only for his "secret faults" did he need Christ's daily free forgiveness, but he declares, "I know that in me, that is in my flesh, dwelleth no good thing: for to will is present with me, but how to perform that which I would I find not." Thus speaks the man to whose holy life we look up with reverent marvel. He does not say that *once* there dwelt no good thing in his flesh;

nor does he mean to say that, irrespective of renewing grace, there dwelt no good in him. He does not reserve the thought, that now indeed he was doing something good before God, but that this had not grown on the soil of his old, but of his new inner man, and was therefore the work of his renewed nature by grace. No; of his own concrete "I" he speaks, who has to acknowledge the flesh as *his* flesh, and the whole inheritance from Adam as *his* inheritance. Of this his sinful flesh, wherein neither ever dwelt, nor now dwells, any good thing, he declares that it hinders him—the renewed Christian—in the performance of the good which he "would" do. So as with ardent desire he sought to do it, so as it must be done to render man righteous before God, from pure delight in obedience, ever disposed to do God's will, and yet never inclined to seek himself in so doing—in short, as Christ the Just One did that which is good: so Paul never did any one out of his many good works. So soon as the slightest thought of self-satisfaction over any done work rose in his mind, though disguised to indiscernibleness by heartfelt thanks to God for his given strength, lo! the commandment would stand at the door, and say, "Thou shalt not covet;" and thus again all was over with his life by the law. "In great things it sufficeth to will them," and most of all in that which is the greatest thing—viz., holiness. But Paul's certainly was no feeble, impotent willing that which is good, after the manner of "good resolves," which ever and anon the law exacts even from unbelievers. No; his life bears other witness! Yet the saint who saw the crown of righteousness laid up for his martyred head falls low at the feet of the righteous Judge, and confesses that by the law giving life only to its fulfillers he ought to be condemned to death, but seizes upon the faithful saying, worthy of all acceptation, that Christ Jesus came into the world to save sinners, "of whom I am chief"—not *was*, but "*am*," (1 Tim. i. 15.) Paul submitted, though not without a groan, to the wretched lot of a never-ceasing, but ever-harassing, war against sin, which—as a robber and rebel against the new man in Christ—continued to dwell in his flesh. To break the iron "law" of contradiction between willing and doing by keeping under his body, in which he certainly was no weakling, (1 Cor. ix. 27,) or to purchase a truce with sin by any "voluntary humility," this he never deemed the work of a Christian man. The law of God which he loved, and the law of sin which he hated—the echoing "Yes" of the inner man to the law in his mind, and Satan's other law in his members, that brought him into captivity to the law of sin—this feeling of unceasing discord within him made him exclaim, "Oh, wretched man that I am! who shall deliver me from the body of this death?" But he went on with "cleansing himself from all filthiness of the flesh and spirit," with "bringing his body into subjection," with "crucifying the flesh with the affections and lusts," with "yielding his members as instruments of righteousness unto God;" in fine, with "perfecting holiness in the fear of God," (2 Cor. vii. 1.) Moreover, he daily experienced that he needed such "going on," as one who had not already attained, neither was already perfect, (Phil. iii. 12;) and that, because the "law" in his members went on with warring and bringing into captivity to the hated service of sin. "So then, with the mind I myself serve the law of God; but with the flesh the law of sin." There the willing service of joy and liberty, here the compulsory service of a hated villanage.

But, imprisoned as yet he was in the body of this death, Paul could sing of deliverance by faith: "I thank God through Jesus Christ our Lord." In one breath he grieves and joys; but the Christian joy got the mastery over the

Christian sorrow, because the spirit triumphed over the flesh. Being found by faith in Christ, and having pardon and acceptance, life and righteousness, conferred by Him, he knows himself free from condemnation, under which unbelievers are held by the law of sin and death. By the indwelling of the Spirit of Christ he knows himself conqueror; in His strength he can renounce the sensual law in his flesh, and become heartily subject to the spiritual law of God; to his mortal body, also, he knows that resurrection and life are secured in Christ. Here, in Rom. viii., he changes his mournful "I" into a joyful "We" and "You." The Christian's woe of sin he has taken on himself; who dares to plead exemption? The Christian's glory he awards to all his brethren in Christ. Finally, after having described the work of the Holy Spirit in believers, and His first-fruits in their hearts, the Spirit's guidance and witness, His adoption and glorious liberty, His expectant hope and comfort under all sufferings of this present time, ending in that song of triumph, the very kernel of the Gospel-nut, "In all these things we are more than conquerors;" he boldly throws the gauntlet of faith at the feet of all powers in heaven and earth, as impotent to separate him from Christ; and with the fullest assurance of final salvation, wherein he was kept to the end, (2 Tim. i. 12,) he exclaims, "I am persuaded, that neither death, nor life, nor angels, nor principalities, nor powers, nor things present, nor things to come, nor height, nor depth, nor any other creature, shall be able to separate us from the love of God, which is in Christ Jesus our Lord." Because he believed, therefore he spoke. His triumphant joy, and the ground of his "more than conqueror's" assurance was Christ, and Christ alone. Upon "God that cannot lie" he knew himself thrown for the hope of eternal life, (Tit. i. 2.) "God is faithful" was his motto for himself and his brethren, with whom he was called unto the fellowship of the Son of God, Jesus Christ our Lord, (1 Cor. i. 9 ; 1 Thess. v. 24.) Because he lived *through grace* by faith in Christ, and ever continued in holy dread lest he should trespass against the operation of the Spirit by applying fragments of His workmanship to the building up again of a legal righteousness, (Gal. ii. 16-21 ;) therefore he could be so sure of his salvation, and free of all doubt to be " without blame before God in love," being " accepted in the Beloved," (Eph. i. 3-7.) Downwards and upwards led his Christian path : down into the deep, where the penitential psalms—these songs, not of the wicked, but of the pious—are experienced ; up to the height, where the psalms of joy—the songs not of angels, but of the just, living by faith—resound. Blessed be " the man of faith," who strengthens his brethren, where he mourns in the deep, where he joys in the height !

"In my heart," says Luther, " reigns and shall reign this one article alone : faith in my dear Lord Jesus Christ, who of all my spiritual and godly thoughts, that ever day or night I may have, is the one only beginning, middle, and end. And yet I find, that of the breadth, and length, and depth, and height of this unbounded, incomprehensible, and infinite wisdom, I scarcely reach a very weak and mean *beginning*, and can hardly bring to light a few small crumbs out of this richest and all-precious mine of gold." Therefore Scripture has given *Hope* as a companion of Faith, stretching forth her eye to that which is perfect and to come, (1 Cor. xiii. 10.)

" Paul's rock of faith was Christ alone,
A trusty shield and weapon,
Who helps us from His heav'nly throne
'Gainst ev'ry ill may happen.
That old malicious foe
Intends us deadly woe,

Arm'd with the strength of hell,
And deepest craft as well;
On earth is not his equal.

" Of our own strength we nothing can,
Straight were we lost for ever;
But for us fights the Son of man,
By God sent to deliver.
Ask ye who this may be?
Christ Jesus named is He,
Of Sabaoth the Lord,
Sole God to be adored;
'Tis He must win the battle."

## VIII.

### THE MAN OF HOPE.

"And for an helmet, the hope of salvation."—1 Thess. v. 8.

Like a warrior decorated with his helmet, which shields his head from the stroke of his adversary, so Paul stands there clad in rich attire, and "rejoicing in hope of the glory of God," (Rom. v. 2,) by which he is armed against every "no," wherewith Satan defies "the armies of the living God," and wherewith things visible and temporal ever seek to oppose the Christian, or to withdraw him from the promises of God. Luther used to call the hope of faith "man's brave heart," and compares the indissoluble pair to the two cherubim upon the mercy-seat. "We are saved by hope," (Rom. viii. 24,) that is, by faith in hope. The salvation we have in Christ we can taste and enjoy on earth only in hope. As in faith, so in hope, Paul "warred a good warfare." Right fitly he is escutcheoned with the sword.

As his preaching and life of faith, so his joy and rejoicing in hope is the bright reflex of his heavenly call, a green branch out of the root of experienced grace. Visibly did the glory of "the second man, the Lord from heaven," (1 Cor. xv. 47,) "shine round about him." But as on the mount of Olives, when the Lord, "while they beheld," was taken up to heaven, and received by a cloud out of their sight, the disciples saw no other light henceforth than that of His word, illuminated by the angel's message, (Acts

i. 9-11;) so did Paul, over his baptism in the house of Judas at Damascus, see no other light than that of Christ's word spoken to him by the mouth of Ananias. Thus he was prepared to testify that Jesus Christ, sitting on God's right hand, and "hid in God," (Col. iii. 1-4,) manifests Himself on earth to faith in His word and sacrament, that Hope, with the eyes of Simeon, beholding his Saviour through the babe's swaddling-clothes, might, through the unveiled veils of the visible means of grace, stretch forth her keen eye unto the heirship of eternal life, (Tit. iii. 7.) As his blessed Saviour, "the Lord of glory," (1 Cor. ii. 8,) had suffered Himself to be persecuted in His poor saints by Saul, so Paul was prepared for a life of tribulation; but as his heavenly Master, "for the joy that was set before Him, endured the cross," (Heb. xii. 2,) so Paul, in hope's anticipation of future bliss with Christ, "reckoned the sufferings of this present time as not worthy to be compared with the glory which shall be revealed in us," (Rom. viii. 18.) On the other hand, his confession was, "If in this life only we have hope in Christ, we are of all men most miserable," (1 Cor. xv. 19.) Israel's King has "endured the cross, and is exalted to His heavenly throne, our great High Priest has completed the sacrifice of Himself," and has entered into His heavenly sanctuary; Israel's Prophet has "preached the kingdom of heaven," and now makes Himself heard through His Spirit in the Church of the Spirit. Hence Paul was constrained to bear witness of Israel's hope of glory, as already fulfilled in Christ, and which, on the day of His glorious appearing, will be accomplished also in His believing people; while the fleshly, exanimate Israel is still pursuing the phantom of her foreshadowed glory. (This is the sum and substance of the Epistle to the Hebrews. \*) "Crucified through weakness,"

\* See note, p. 95.—Tr.

—viz., "in the likeness of sinful flesh,"—Christ now ever "liveth by the power of God," (2 Cor. xiii. 4.) Therefore Paul set all things that "might have been gain" on "knowing Him, and the power of His resurrection, and the fellowship of His sufferings, being made conformable unto His death; if by any means he might attain unto the resurrection of the dead," (Phil. iii. 10, 11.) "As sorrowful" in the world and in the flesh, "yet always rejoicing," (2 Cor. vi. 10,) because "rejoicing in hope;" this is the Christian's calling and enviable lot, (Rom. xii. 12.)

"Jesus Christ is our hope," he writes to Timothy, (1 Tim. i. 1,) and before the Colossians he unfolds the heavenly "riches of the glory of this mystery among the Gentiles;" and then, gathering all its treasure into a golden nutshell, he extols its incalculable value to them in these words: "which [mystery] is Christ in you, the hope of glory," (Col. i. 27.) Everywhere the Apostle manifests his gladsome confidence that the Church of Christ, though hoping for His glorious reappearing, yet enjoys through all time His gracious presence on earth; for He has said, "Lo, I am with you alway, even unto the end of the world." Therefore he hopes for no future glory which is not pledged and sealed to believers by the Spirit of Christ dwelling in them. "Where the Spirit of the Lord is, there is liberty," (2 Cor. iii. 17.) Thus we are freed from the bondage of corruption, while looking for the glorious liberty of the children of God; and having the "first-fruits of the Spirit," we wait for the adoption, to wit, the redemption of our body, (Rom. viii. 21, 23,) a confession of hope both humble and bold. No less than St John is Paul penetrated with the idea of the present reality of eternal life to and in Christ's believing people. The mind of them both is expressed in these words (of A. H. Francke:)—

> "Farewell, what's called day and year,
> Eternity is round me here;
> Because I live in Jesus."

To express what a Christian man has and is in Christ, St Paul is particularly fond of the words "riches," "perfection," "fulness." Sevenfold in one sentence he pours forth his praise of the all-sufficient and all-abounding riches of God's grace, (2 Cor. ix. 8.) To be "filled with all the fulness of God," is his prayer for the faithful in Christ Jesus at Ephesus, (2 Cor. iii. 19.) To "present every man perfect in Christ Jesus," thereunto he laboured, striving according to His working, which worked in him mightily, (Col. i. 28, 29.) But as humbly as St John confesses, "Behold, now are we the sons of God, and it does not yet appear what we shall be," (1 John iii. 2,) does he feel reconciled to the veiled state of expectant hope, wherein the life and salvation of believers is yet hid; although as ardent in anticipation he already calls them "the first-fruits of the Spirit." As the first sheaves of the harvest in the holy land were offered to the Lord for a wave-offering in token that the entire harvest was due to Him as a thank-offering; so we, who are the Israel of the Gospel, go on boldly waving the Spirit's first-fruits to and fro, to all ends of the earth, and up to heaven, when we sing and say, "Here all sins forgiven are."* He that by faith enjoys and confesses this "good of the land," (Isa. i. 19,) —to wit, of the Christian Church,—possesses in this one royal gift of the Spirit the entire inheritance of promise in hope; and, putting under foot death and the grave, can triumphantly exclaim, "My flesh too shall live again. This life past, there is for me a life throughout eternity. Amen."

Is Jesus Christ the hope of believers? then all God's

---
* Lofty! but dark to me.—Tr.

promises in Him are Yea and Amen,—"unto the glory of God by us," adds the Apostle, (2 Cor. i. 20.) " By us "—viz., by the evangelical ministers and witnesses of Jesus Christ, the Son of God, (2 Cor. v. 19.) With the advent of Christ and His accomplished work of redemption, and His coming in the Spirit, preaching peace to far and nigh, (Eph. ii. 17,) the last time of the history of salvation has set in, which continues from the day of Pentecost to that of the Lord's coming again in glory. "The ends of the world are come" upon us, (1 Cor. x. 11.) In the last epoch of days (wherewith the last period of time, and heaven's kingdom on earth began) has God "spoken unto us by His Son," (Heb. i. 2,) whom He sent forth, when the fulness of the time was come, (Gal. iv. 4.) Thus the Apostle views the historical progress of God's kingdom in the world, and finds Israel's fundamental hope, that Abraham "should be the heir of the world," (Rom. iv. 13,) unfolded by the prophetic word, and completely fulfilled in Him who is of Abraham's seed—viz., in the One who is the first-born among many brethren, (Rom. viii. 29; Gal. iii. 29.) Living then, as he did, at dawn of the evangelical day, Paul anticipated with joyous hope the approach of noontide, at which the glory of the Son of man would shine into, and illuminate, as by flashes of lightning, the world's midnight darkness. He was glad when a year, and again another, had passed of the Church's time of suffering, which himself helped to shorten by the filling-up measure of his own, (Col. i. 24.) Upon the nearly twenty years which lay between his conversion and departure from Corinth he looked back, not tired of his labour and sufferings, but with growing joy of the now nearer approached salvation, (Rom. xiii. 11.) We must not think that at one time (1 Thess. iv. 15-17) he expected to live till the Lord's return, and that at another (2 Thess. ii.) he had relinquished this hope. He ever felt the last day as so near that he did not put it off to any measured distance, by reckoning years and days which would have to elapse, or events which would have to come to pass, before the end should come. With joyous longing, mixed with holy dread, he was himself prepared for the Lord's coming; and also strengthened the expectations of the faithful in what they knew perfectly well—"that the day of the Lord would so come as a thief in the night," (1 Thess. v. 1, &c.) With a "Maran-atha"—"the Lord cometh"—he greets the lukewarm at Corinth, (1 Cor. xvi. 22;) and woe to him who should have returned this greeting with a confident "Not yet." A short while after his First Epistle to the Thessalonians, where, "by the word of the Lord," he gives expression to the blessed hope of the dead, by saying that "we which are alive and remain unto the coming of the Lord shall not prevent them which are asleep"—(mark well, in this he speaks the mind of all Christians that are "at home in the body," now as well as then, who, beside the graves of their loved ones "which are asleep," have to take it for their comfort, until such "we" be ended in the last-born children of Christ's Church)—shortly after this consolatory epistle, Paul wrote his second to the Thessalonians. He had heard that certain spiritualists had subtilised his doctrine of the Lord's advent, and of the gathering of the faithful unto Him, into the saying that "the day of Christ is already at hand," (2 Thess. ii. 2;) similarly as afterwards Hymenæus and Philetus converted his doctrine of the resurrection of the flesh into the frivolous saying that "the resurrection is past already," (2 Tim. ii. 18.) This (2 Thess. ii. 2) had terrified the young Christians at Thessalonica. Therefore the Apostle comforts them with the assurance that their gathering together unto Christ was but an earnest of the brightness of His coming; that then the days of their sufferings would be ended. But he reminds them also of what he had told them from the beginning, that the fall of the unbelieving Jews was but the prelude to the falling away in the midst of the Church, which would come when " he who now letteth " and " will let" (the authorities ordained by God) should be taken out of the way, and he "who opposeth and exalteth himself above all that is called God "—*i.e.*, antichrist clad in worldly power under spiritual show—should "sit in the temple of God." This "man of sin," the "son of perdition," in whom, as its head, the mystery of iniquity becomes concentrated, will develop itself in opposition to the true Church, whose head is Christ—hardly, therefore, in a single individual, but in a succession of bearers of the antichristian spirit— "whom the Lord shall consume with the spirit of His mouth, and shall destroy with the brightness of His coming," (2 Thess. ii. 1-8.) How then? did the prophetic certainty, that before the day of Christ's coming antichrist must be revealed, hinder Paul from living in such nearness of the last day, that, if it pleased God, he might greet its appearance on this side the grave? By no means. If so, he would have recalled in the second what he had written in the first epistle. Floating before his hopeful eyes he beheld the call of all nations by the Gospel, (Rom. x. 18,) himself cheerfully running his course as a Gospel minister, " to fulfil the word of God," (Col. i. 25;) the net was filling with fishes, and daily he saw the end draw nearer, the preaching of the Gospel for a witness unto all nations, (Matt. xxiv. 14; Col. i. 6, 23.) He dared not to measure the days, neither those of the Lord's patience before the day of His wrath, nor those of the Church's suffering before that of her deliverance; but of this he always was sure, that the hope laid up for believers in heaven (Col. i. 5) suffered no delay by unfulfilled prophecies, for either they had received, or were constantly now receiving, their fulfilment in the Gospel. Whether antichrist be revealed at Jerusalem, or Rome, or Thessalonica, or any other place, he certainly must be revealed "in the temple of God," which Paul was building up by the preaching of the Gospel. It was not surely against far-off enemies, but very near present ones, that he called his brethren to arms, putting on the breastplate of faith, and for an helmet the hope of salvation, (1 Thess. v. 8; Eph. vi. 10, &c.)

But must not the fall of the Jewish nation, and their promised final salvation, defer the coming of the Lord in His glory? Those that make Paul wait for a general conversion of the Jews, in a far distant time, do not in truth comprehend his hope of the last day being near. But Romans xi. teaches the contrary, if otherwise we understand, in some measure, the mystery of the hope of Israel in connexion with the whole apostolic doctrine, and in the light of the prophetic word.[*] It is in the Gospel Church of Christ, the heiress to Israel's promise, that Paul sees the broken-off branches of the olive-tree strike leaves again and bear fruit. Those of Israel who are not Israel, because forsaking their stem, "the root of Jesse" promised to their fathers, (Isa. i. 1, 10,) they are not partakers of the root and fatness of the good olive-tree—are broken off. But, lo! their fall is the riches of the Gentiles; their casting away the reconciling of the world. The graffing in of the wild branches into the good olive tree—the rearing and growth of the Gentile Church—is brought about more speedily than the Apostle had thought, when still bent on winning the Jews, in order to prepare them for becoming the missionary nation of the world. Nevertheless, God has

---

[*] We can here find space only to some lines of the picture he has drawn in that chapter. In my "Bible Lessons" on the Romans I have attempted to elucidate more at large the meaning and bearing of that much-disputed question.

thoughts of mercy even over the broken-off branches. Was not Paul himself one of them? and has not God shewed in him that He is indeed able to graff them in' again? Yea, and in raising up this shoot of Benjamin to be a chosen vessel of Christ, the King of Israel, has He not shewn that "His gifts and calling are without repentance?" For has not this Israelite's calling brought "life from the dead" to the world, which he visited with the word of reconciliation when cast out from Jerusalem? Therefore, it well beseemed him to hope that the growth and extension of the good olive-tree, planted for the life of the world, would be incalculably promoted by the re-acceptance and re-graffing into it of his own brethren. Though the fulfilment of this hope remained far behind Paul's ardent wishes, yet did he not therefore mistake the power of God, who, in face of the unbelieving mass, continues His goodness to them that abide not in unbelief; "they shall be graffed in; for God is able to graff them in again." But this He will do in the order of His grace, which, through the fall of the Jews, the outward historical people of Israel, has taken this turn, that the fallen ones are to be provoked to jealousy by the Gentiles being brought into the salvation of Israel. It is not God's will that they should remain lying on the ground; therefore He follows them with wonders and signs of His wrath, but a wrath in which He remembers mercy. Into no tree of any other nationality shall the broken-off branches from Israel's own be graffed; but rather Moses' curse and our Saviour's word, "This generation shall not pass away till all be fulfilled," (Luke xxi. 32,) is to bear them distinct from other nations through all generations to the end, in order that their forlorn condition as broken-off branches may constantly remind them of their faithlessness to "the root of Jesse," "which shall stand for an ensign of the people," and to which the Gentiles shall seek, (Isa. xi. 10.)

And so long as the graffing of Gentile branches into the olive-tree of the Gospel Church lasts, so long also the graffing in again of Jewish branches into their own olive-tree shall continue. This is Paul's hope. "Blindness in part is happened to Israel." Among the whole mass hardened in unbelief "there is a remnant according to the election of grace," whose graffing in again will fill up the number of the saved, and constitute the fulness of the won ones of Israel. "Until the fulness of the Gentiles be come in," God will not cease to call and draw the cast-off "children of the kingdom" by the voice of their national home, that He may woo them back to His people, which He hath not cast off, but hath kept all His promises with them in Christ Jesus, the seed of Abraham. "And *so*," (Rom. xi. 26,) not otherwise,—not as the Jews, proud of their fleshly descent fancy, —"all Israel shall be saved;" the fulness of the Gentiles, together with that of the returned Jews; the entire fulness of the *true* Israel, all branches found in the olive-tree by faith, as well the new graffed as the old ones graffed in again. Such hope, grounded in the mystery of Christ and His Church, Paul finds confirmed by the prophetic word: "As it is written, There shall come out of Sion the Deliverer, and shall turn away ungodliness from Jacob. For this is my covenant with them, when I shall take away their sins." From two prophetic passages, (Isa. lix. 20, xxviii. 9,) and two prophetic psalm words, (Ps. xiv. 7, cx. 2,) the Apostle collects his Scripture proof, that out of the Gospel Church, as Zion's legitimate daughter, the Deliverer comes, arrayed with Gentile sons and daughters, whom He hath washed and sanctified in His blood, to provoke them who "by nature" are Israel, or *Jacob*, to vie with these in coming to the marriage of their liege Lord; and *so* all Israel be saved. God's "new covenant" in Christ "with the house of Israel" is: "I will forgive their iniquity, and remember their sins no more," (Jer. xxxi. 31-34;) and the word "when" (Rom. xi. 27)—when I shall take away their sins —does not certainly point to a far distant time, that shall not begin "until the fulness of the Gentiles be come in :" but rather through the whole time of the New Covenant the testament is in force, which was opened, when the seed came, to whom the promise was made, (Gal. iii. 19;) and so long, till the Deliverer be come to the last child of the Gentiles, will He also continue to come to Israel after the flesh, which hath wrested the testament of grace by works, that He may "turn away ungodliness from Jacob.". Did not Paul's own experience testify to the fulfilment of this prophetic word? Therefore his hope for Israel rested on the ground that "the gifts and calling of God are without repentance." Out of Zion, built up at Damascus, did the Deliverer come to him, turning away from this son of Jacob, of the tribe of Benjamin, the ungodliness which had shut him out from Israel's glorious hope; and being washed from his sins by the blood of the everlasting covenant, he staked his life on the admission of the Gentiles into the tents of Zion; yet not to bring them alone into Jerusalem's prosperity, but also to see the crown of his hope bloom upon the head of Zion's King and His chosen people, and so *all* Israel be saved. The "lastlings" will be saved no otherwise than the "firstlings." The mystery of the hope of Israel is a mystery of grace and of faith, and like all mysteries of God "without controversy great" in the Church.

As the progressive development of God's kingdom to the end of time, so likewise the future glory of it presents itself to Paul's hope, as resulting from the grace of which all believers have become partakers in Jesus Christ. Those that have "the testimony of Christ confirmed" in them "come behind in no gift," but "are enriched by Him" in everything, while "waiting for the coming of our Lord Jesus Christ," (1 Cor. i. 4-7.) Quite in Paul's sense says Augustine, "Ask no man for it, turn to thine own heart; already art thou placed at God's right hand. Do not mind thy glory being hidden; when the Lord cometh, thou shalt appear with Him in glory. The root liveth, though the branch appear withered; inwardly, in the living marrow, is already the strength of the leaves and fruit, but they wait for the summer." What in reversion is given unto us in Christ Jesus, the Crucified and Risen again, "God hath revealed unto us by His Spirit," (1 Cor. ii. 9, &c.,) that with enlightened eyes of our understanding we may know what is the hope of His calling, and what the riches of the glory of His inheritance in the saints, and what is the exceeding greatness of His power to us-ward who believe. From the believer's "*I am*" Christ's by faith, hope draws her "*I shall be*" glorified with Him. The Christian, in whose heart God hath shined, sees "the light of the glory of God in the face of Jesus Christ," (2 Cor. iv. 6.) In Him we are "sealed with the Holy Spirit of promise, which is the earnest of our inheritance until the redemption of the purchased possession, unto the praise of His glory," (Eph. i. 13, 14.) "Now we see through a glass, darkly; but then face to face: now I know in part; but then shall I know, even as also I am known," (1 Cor. xiii. 12.) The heavenly blessings, wherewith we are blessed in Christ, we cannot now see but "through a glass," conveying a reflection of them to us clad in the form of "human speech," (Rom. vi. 19.) "Darkly," (more literally, "in enigmas,") we read of them in God's Word, yet plainly enough, yea, in our present state only thereby clear, that it speaks to us in pictures and signs, wherewith the Holy Ghost represents the incarnation and humanity of the Son of God. When we shall behold Him, the glorified Son of man, face to face, then shall cease the reflection of His grace and truth in human speech; which is like a cloud in sunshine, full of light on the other side, yet throwing shade on us below. "Done away" shall be "that which is in part," our present knowing in part, wherein we possess the truth only by bringing into captivity our reason to the obedience of Christ, whereby every enigma of apparent contradiction in Christian doctrine is solved, or rather submitted to by faith, because it has with it the hope of one day beholding, as it were, in a perfect panorama, the harmonious solution of the whole. As we were known of God, when in Christ He drew us to Himself, and received us into the blessed fellowship of His love, so we shall also know Him with the clear eyes of love, when, "conformed to the image of His Son," (Rom. viii. 29,) we shall stand at His right hand. Here the Holy Ghost, through the word of faith, begets and nourishes the new man, there only he comes to perfection, "unto the measure of the stature of the fulness of Christ," (Eph. iv. 13.) Faith makes of children men that are not tossed to and fro with every wind of doctrine; but hope points to a manhood compared to which Paul himself was but a lisping child: "When I was a child, I spake as a child, I understood as a child, I thought as a child; but when I became a man, I put away childish things," (1 Cor. xiii. 11.) Together with Christian knowledge the Christian will also reaches forth to perfection in hope. Paul could do all things through Christ strengthening him, (Phil. iv. 13;) yet could he do so only in hot warfare against the sin in his flesh, which lay encamped between will and deed, and stamped its Adamite seal upon all the thoughts, words, and works of his inner man. Even there, where he shines forth in the perfect righteousness of Christ by faith, (Phil. iii. 9,) he also expresses his ardent longing after perfection in the blessed kingdom of his risen Redeemer, and then continues: "Not as though I had already attained, either were already perfect; but I follow after, if that I may apprehend that, for which also I am apprehended of Christ Jesus." Yea, right brotherly he takes his beloved Philippians by the hand, and, putting himself with them in rank and file of the Christian race, he says, "Brethren, I count not myself to have apprehended: but this one thing I do, forgetting those things which are behind, and reaching forth unto those things which are before, I press toward the mark for the prize of the high calling of God in Christ Jesus," (Phil. iii. 12-14.) "I shall win it, what's the wager?" was the holy challenge of his faith to his hope. In the same way he represents himself to the Corinthians as a holy racer, who stakes all on winning the crown, (1 Cor. ix. 24-27.) Altogether he is very fond of viewing his whole life as a great spiritual warfare, (2 Cor. x. 2-5.) "Enduring hardness, as a good soldier of Jesus Christ," he always lies in the field straining every nerve to gain the prize, which is eternal life, purchased by Christ's blood, given out of pure grace to faith, and laid hold of for their honour, glory, and immortality, by those who, by patient continuance in welldoing, seek for such end of their hope, (Rom. ii. 7.) "Fight the good fight of faith," he exhorts his Timothy, "lay hold on eternal life, whereunto thou art also called, and hast professed a good profession before many witnesses," (1 Tim. vi. 12.) Coupled with his unshaken certainty of salvation is the holy fear of a man in Christ, who cannot earn, but may lose his salvation, and be finally "a castaway," (1 Cor. ix. 27.) "Cast not away your confidence," we hear him say to those whose hope, as an anchor of the soul, both sure and steadfast, (Heb. vi. 19,) was in danger of being thrown away on earthly things. To escape this danger, and keep it centred in Jesus, who ascended up to heaven, he thus encourages and exhorts them: "Cast not away therefore your confidence, which hath great recompence of reward. For ye have need of patience, that, after ye have done the will of God, ye might receive the promise. For yet a little while, and He that shall come will come, and will not tarry. Now, the just shall live by faith: but if any man draw back, my soul shall have no pleasure in him, saith the Lord. But we are not of them who draw back unto perdition; but of them that believe to the saving of the soul," (Heb. x. 35-39.) Christ certainly refreshes His faithful followers with joy and peace already in this life, and we have seen Paul's heart abound in Christian joy. Still, every blessing he enjoyed in faith was only a foretaste to him of the heavenly joy his ardent soul anticipated in hope: "To me to live is Christ, and to die is gain," he writes in that letter of joy and love to the Philippians. "I am in a strait betwixt two, having a desire to depart, and to be with Christ, which is far better," (Phil. i. 21, &c.) The longer he lived in "this tabernacle," the more ardent became his desire "to be absent from the body, and to be present with the Lord," (2 Cor. v. 1-8.) To the Romans, where he most extols the treasure of a life by faith, he couches his last wishes and blessings in these words: "Now, the God of peace fill you with all joy and peace in believing, that ye may abound in hope through the power of the Holy Ghost," (Rom. xv. 13.) Not less firmly and constantly than Peter, whom the Church of old has designated as "the man of hope," does Paul keep his eye fixed on the heavenly inheritance, and on that day in which, at the glorious appearing of Jesus Christ, whom his soul loveth, the believer will rejoice with joy unspeakable, and full of glory, (1 Pet. i. 3-9.)

"Flesh and blood cannot inherit the kingdom of God,"

(1 Cor. xv. 50,) and yet the heirs of the kingdom are men having flesh and blood. Far from depreciating the body, (Col. ii. 23,) which rather he designates as "the temple of the Holy Ghost," (1 Cor. vi.19,) Paul felt the more grievously its fleshly and death-doomed condition, and therefore groaned under its burden, (2 Cor. v. 4.) But he also comforted himself with the hope he had for his mortal body in Christ's own, the Risen One, whom he had beheld in heavenly glory. "For we are members of His body, of His flesh, and of His bones," (Eph. v. 30,) he says of the Church, which Christ, by His word and sacrament, sanctifieth, cleanseth, nourisheth, and cherisheth, "that it should be holy and without blemish." He views the Spirit of Christ in believers as an earnest also of the life of their mortal bodies, (Rom. viii. 11,) and therefore waits for the complete adoption, (ib. ver. 23,) when God shall recognise as His dear children the brethren of "the first-born from the dead," (Col. i. 18;) for "the Saviour of the body," (Eph. v. 23,) the Lord Jesus Christ, "shall change our vile body, that it may be fashioned like unto His glorious body, according to the working, whereby He is able to subdue all things unto Himself," (Phil. iii. 21.) For redemption, not *from*, but *of* the body Paul hopes. His arduous conflict in the mortal body did indeed extort from him the doleful exclamation: "O wretched man that I am! who shall deliver me from the body of this death?" But in the triumphant chapter that follows it the hope breaks forth, that even this mortal body shall also be delivered from the bondage of corruption. "The resurrection of the flesh" was, indeed, an article of most solemn importance with the Apostle. The naked "immortality of the soul" never was any object of his hope. Though death he deemed gain, because to die in the service of Christ, and for His name, was joy and honour to him; yet it was not to be

"unclothed," but "clothed upon," that he longed for, (2 Cor. v. 1, &c.) With confident hope he looked forward to the dissolution of "the earthly house of this tabernacle;" for of the "eternal house"—the future risen body—he could say, "We have a building of God, an house not made with hands," because this "building" and "house" is pledged to the believer in the body of his risen Head and Saviour in heaven, to whom His members will and must be joined. Yet the monster Death was an object of horror to him; not that he dreaded its terrors,—them he had conquered through faith in Christ's death and victorious rising again,—but he shuddered at the last enemy's ruthless onslaught on Christ's members, clad as they are in their Saviour's righteousness and life. His was that groaning over death to which Jesus was moved on proceeding to Lazarus's grave, (John xi. 33-38.) It was the mournful reflection of the grim tyrant's murderous right over man created in God's image, and redeemed through Christ's blood. Fain would he have seen "the last enemy" robbed of his prey. "For in this," he says, "we groan, earnestly desiring to be clothed upon with our house which is from heaven. For we that are in this tabernacle do groan being burdened; not for that we would be unclothed, but clothed upon, that mortality might be swallowed up in life,"—swallowed up as the sun consumes the fog,—so that in the twinkling of an eye this corruptible may be "changed into incorruptible, and this mortal into immortality," (1 Cor. xv. 51, &c.; 1 Thess. iv. 17.) Yet, if it must be so, Paul also is resigned to pass, through bitter death, from his earthly pilgrimage to his heavenly home with the Lord, where faith shall cease, and hope be lost in sight. "For our light affliction, which is but for a moment," was his challenge just before (2 Cor. iv. 17, 18) to the murderer and destroyer, "worketh for us"—by trying the Christian faith, and putting to test his hope—"a far more exceeding and eternal weight of glory; while we look not at the things which are seen, but at those which are not seen; for the things which are seen are temporal, but the things which are not seen are eternal." The eye of faith, called hope, will be rewarded —in yonder blessed sight—with an eternal weight of glory, for having "looked" at things which are not seen, which is folly to sense and reason, (Heb. xi. 27.) And what makes to us the invisible so incontestably sure, in a world so strangely the opposite to all our hope? "He that wrought us for the self-same thing is God, who also hath given unto us the earnest of the Spirit," (2 Cor. v. 5.)

The celebrated chapter, wherein Paul most joyfully confesses his hope of a glorious resurrection, (1 Cor. xv.,) we have already adverted to; but let us have the pleasure of expatiating upon it more fully. By him also, as "the least of the apostles," the risen Saviour hath been seen, and though "last of all," yet, by the grace of God, he became the foremost in preaching His Gospel. "Now, if Christ be preached, that He rose from the dead, how say some among you that there is no resurrection of the dead?" Who will dare to tear asunder the Head and His members? Those wiseacres who think it folly to believe in a resurrection of the dead, must also have the courage to deny that Christ rose from the dead. But if Christ be not risen, then all Christian faith is vain, and all evangelical preaching is a worthless thing; then the apostles are "false witnesses," sin is unatoned, "they also which are fallen asleep in Christ are perished," being slain by unconquered death, and those that have been deceived into devoting their life to a dead Christ are worse off than those who have adorned theirs with "elysian flowers," or dwelt in "amaranthine bowers." "But now—O blessed *now!*—is

Christ risen from the dead, and become the first-fruits of them that slept." In the word "first-fruits" lies the Christian's anchor of hope. Paul loves, as we have seen by a glance at Romans v., to place Adam and Christ in counter-position; Adam the sad beginner of a mortal race, Christ the triumphant restorer of a new and immortal race. And as there he does it in praise of the universal grace of life, which exults in the universal judgment over death, so also here. The universal defeat of mankind in Adam he sees reversed by the universal victory in Christ. The perverse talk of a "universal restoration" (*apocatastasis*,) fain hoped for by some, has, like all erroneous doctrine, laid the egg of error into the nest of truth. Death's universal reign by Adam's transgression has, indeed, been broken and conquered for all by Christ's victory over it in rising from the dead, and becoming "the first-fruits of them that slept;" but like "as in Adam all die," because, born of the flesh, they are partakers of Adam's nature, "so in Christ shall all be made alive," because, born of the Spirit, they are made partakers of Christ's grace by faith. These only Paul has here in view, while those who through their unbelief are eliminated from man's redemption, have no share in the blessed resurrection to eternal life described in this chapter. They shall indeed "come forth" also,— for "all that are in their graves shall hear His voice,"— but alas! "unto the resurrection of damnation," and not unto that of eternal bliss, (John v. 28, 29.) It was at this that Felix trembled. Christ our Head is risen, but in the members no resurrection is yet visible. Nevertheless the Apostle exhorts them that are baptized into Christ's death, and walk in newness of life, to "reckon themselves to be dead indeed unto sin, but alive unto God through Jesus Christ our Lord," (Rom. vi. 11.) But it costs the total renunciation of self and its natural perception, to reckon ourselves as grown together in the likeness of Christ's resurrection. Therefore Paul bids the Christian to strengthen his hope by "looking" at the things which are "not seen," unpuzzled by this sacred oxymoron; and teaches us to apprehend that holy order, "Christ the first-fruits, afterward they that are Christ's at His coming." No sooner than on the glorious day of His coming again shall the entire harvest follow their great First-fruit, in springing up and blooming forth from their graves. Of a "first" and "second" resurrection—that *before* and this *on* the last day—Paul knows nothing; so we may take the "first resurrection" (Rev. xx. 5, 6) to mean none other than that which faith celebrates over the baptismal grave, (Col. ii. 12;) and the thousand years' reign of the confessors of Christ, the reign which Christ's Spirit is exercising through the Gospel over all nations that do homage to Him. By "then cometh the end," Paul does not mean the universal resurrection of the just and unjust, as following that of " the thousand years' reign;" but he thus explains what he means by "the end:" "When He shall have delivered up the kingdom to God, even the Father; when He shall have put down all rule, and all authority and power." This surrender of the finished reign of grace to God the Father will take place when, to the very last of them, (Heb. ii. 14,) the Son of His love shall have put all enemies under His feet; and thus the prediction of the Son of Man in the eighth Psalm (cf. Heb. i., ii.) be brought to its fulfilment in the restored reign of mankind through their Representative and "Captain of their salvation." When Christ's word from the cross— " It is finished!"—shall find its re-echo in, " All things are put under His feet," all, with one single exception—viz., Him who did put all things under Him; then the end shall have come, whereunto from the beginning the whole history of salvation tended; and "then shall the Son also

Himself be subject unto Him that put all things under Him, that God may be all in all." Until this glorious issue Christ our King sways the sceptre of His power in heaven and earth, as the Mediator between God and men, (1 Tim. ii. 5,) in order to free mankind, held bound by Satan, sin, and death, and through the "joyful tidings" of His accomplished redemption, to lead them back to communion with God. Only when, through His office of grace, God shall have become again all in all, and every antagonistic power shall have been cast out from His kingdom—only then it is that the Son delivers it up to the Father. Yet in doing so He does not give it out of His hand. "Whose kingdom shall have no end," is the confession of His Church, and rightly so. As before the foundation of the world the Son was throned with the Father, equal God in honour and might, so will Jesus Christ throughout eternity sit upon the throne of His glory, to which He will exalt also all the Father hath given Him; and every tongue shall confess that Jesus Christ is the Lord, to the glory of God the Father, (Phil. ii. 11.) In Him all have now become subject to God the Father; the "First-fruit" of now glorified mankind has drawn all after and to Him; the eternal Son of God, who is very man, rules from everlasting to everlasting, as Head of His Church, reigning with Him, (2 Tim. ii. 12,) and whose reign in Him will be in blessed subjection to God. Such is the goal of the Church; and she is sure of this glorious goal, because Christ is risen from the dead. Death has become a derision to them who are "baptized over the dead"—the bodies of the blessed martyrs, (or thus: who have insured their dying bodies in baptism unto life,) who do not count their lives dear unto themselves, but live unto Him who died for them and rose again; who count themselves as sheep for the slaughter, (Rom. viii. 36;) who bear about in their bodies the dying of the Lord Jesus, (2 Cor. iv. 10;) yea, who die daily, that they may gain for their joy and crown of rejoicing (1 Thess. ii. 19, 20) those that are made alive by their preaching. On whose side will ye be now, O Corinthians? on Paul's? or of those who, denying our Christian hope, are only consistent when they say, "Let us eat and drink, for tomorrow we die?" Whatever their talk may be of "God," it can beguile no sober-minded Christian; for to whom the resurrection from the dead is naught, their God is naught. With such men Paul will have nothing to do, while he gladly answers the question of timid Christians, "How are the dead raised up? and with what body do they come?" Behold the mystery of resurrection portrayed in the dying and sprouting grain, of the rising body in the manifold riches of celestial and terrestrial bodies. Should the Almighty be at a loss how to form the bodies of the raised? Interpreting by the emblem of the grain, the Apostle says, "So also is the resurrection of the dead. It is sown in corruption, it is raised in incorruption; it is sown in dishonour, it is raised in glory; it is sown in weakness, it is raised in power; in fine, it is sown a natural (*i.e.*, in the original—a *psychical*) body, it is raised a spiritual body." Psychical is the body that is interred, because *psyche*—the soul—pervading it, holds it together; and, according to Scripture language, animals have this soul in common with man, only that man's soul, since the fall, has become sinful, and the souled body "natural" to man, and liable to death because of sin, (Rom. viii. 10;) but the spirit, which, through the indwelling of the Holy Ghost, has become life, will finally pervade again both body and soul with His power, as now the material body is pervaded by the soul. As there is a psychical body, so there is also a spiritual body, which exists, first-fruit-like, in Christ. From the first Adam, as our earthly progenitor, we have the psychical

K

body, whose living soul, through the spirit's fall from God, has become fleshly, animal, mortal; the spiritual body we receive from Christ, "the Lord from heaven," who—as the "last Adam"—"was made quickening Spirit through His resurrection," and who now—sacramentally and spiritually —engrafts His heavenly life into His people, (John vi. 54, 63,) in order to crown His work of love in them by raising, at the last day, their "sown" psychical bodies to living spiritual bodies. In anticipation already of this glorious change, the Apostle says, "As we have borne the image of the earthy, we shall also bear the image of the heavenly;" that is, with body and soul glorified, we shall be "changed into the same image with Him from glory to glory, even as by the Spirit of the Lord," (2 Cor. iii. 18.) There indeed the Apostle will shine with resplendent glory, yet by the splendour of the same light which shall give perfect bliss also to the meanest of his co-redeemed brethren. Flesh and blood, now corruptible, shall then incorruptibly belong to the spirits of the just made perfect; after the same manner as to the Son of God belong His flesh and blood, which now are the Christian's meat and drink. How constantly expectant Paul was of "the last trump," not only when writing to the Thessalonians, (1 Thess. iv. 13, &c.,) but also, when penning this chapter of hope, we see from his repeating here as "a mystery" (ver. 51, &c.) what there he communicated as "the word of the Lord:" "The trumpet shall sound, and the dead shall be raised incorruptible, and we shall be changed"—viz., we whom the last day meets alive in corruptible bodies. Thus he could say, because the sound of the *last* trump was near to him in that of the *first*—viz., the Gospel (John v. 25, 28;) while at the same time he was prepared to die. "God hath both raised up the Lord," he writes in this same Epistle (chap. vi. 14,) "and will also raise up us by His own power," (cf. 2 Cor. iv. 14.)

Changed from corruptible into incorruptible all men must be, whether it be by being raised, or "clothed upon;" for without this change the "joint-heirs with Christ" cannot inherit the kingdom with Him. But this they shall as surely as, through Christ's victory over death and hell, they have the first-fruits of His Spirit; and their complete victory with Him shall finally accomplish the prophetic word, which the Holy Spirit re-echoes in full gospel triumph through Paul, "Death is swallowed up in victory!" (Isa. xxv. 8.) "O death, where is thy sting? O grave, where is thy victory?" (Hos. xiii. 14.)

One thing yet remains to complete the picture of the man of hope. In the Christian's earthly that shall become heavenly, after the similitude of Christ's glorified body, the Apostle finds a pledge of the whole creation becoming glorified. In that song of songs of his, (Rom. viii.,) which we heard the man of *faith* sing, his *hope* also raises her voice to the highest pitch. The mockers of our Christian hope, the persecutors of a flock whose Head is in heaven, are walking the way of the children of Cain, and, looking only on the things which are seen, regale themselves with the pleasures of this world, finding both their honour and delight in them. There now comes Paul forth with quite a new kind of joy, to the comfort of all his companions in tribulation. The very creature, idolised by the ungodly, and applied by them for the adorning (κός- μος) of their cheerless wretchedness, the Apostle gives to the poor Christian, who yet is the expectant heir of glory, as a companion of his suffering and hope, by "drawing," as Luther expresses it, "the holy cross through every creature, and making heaven and earth, and all things therein, suffer with us." But he also looks forward with delight to the day of their redemption—the day when all created beings, now our joint-prisoners in mortal body, shall also lay aside their menial garb, worn as by bondmen, and be clad in festive holiday attire. "For the earnest expectation of the creature waited for the manifestation of the sons of God. For the creature was made subject to vanity, not willingly, but by reason of Him who hath subjected the same in hope; because the creature itself also shall be delivered from the bondage of corruption into the glorious liberty of the children of God. For we know that the whole creation groaneth and travaileth in pain together until now," (Rom. viii. 19-22.) It is said by Jewish Rabbis in praise of Saul's teacher, Gamaliel, that he was not versed only in their holy writings and heathen literature, but that also he understood the language of creation. Paul, however, was initiated into its mysterious import by another teacher. We have heard him speak at Lystra (Acts xiv. 15-17) and Athens (Acts xvii. 24, &c.) of the rich blessings distributed with kindly hand by the beneficent Creator and patient Preserver of all things; and he leaves the Gentiles without excuse if they perceive not His power and goodness manifested in His creation, (Rom. i. 19, 20.) From his native province, Cilicia, with all its fruitful plains on the foot of "Taurus," and its jessamine and oleander shrubs on the banks of the "Cydnus," onward to the charming regions of Campania, he has listened to land and sea. The hills about Jerusalem and the flower-studded brooks of the Holy Land, the cedars of Lebanon and the majestic palm of Syria, the olive groves of Attica and the evergreen pines of Corinth, the motley group of isles in the Greek Archipelago and the sunny splendour of their vine-covered hills—all the sublime beauties and lovely grace of nature found in Paul an attentive and fond observer. But he heard heaven and earth tell of something else than do poets and natural philosophers, when they listen to "the tales of the wood."

Yea, better than his honoured teacher Gamaliel could do it, did the holy prophets lead him to view nature, after their light had dawned on him in the person of Christ. He now understood the 8th Psalm, because he knew man as the fallen, but in Christ restored, lord "over the works of God's hand." In the man made of earth, the creature had her share in the honour of the Divine image. When man's spirit was darkened by Satan's, and his psychical body became a prey to death, the living light of creation expired, the tie between the visible and invisible world was rent, every creature was "made subject to vanity," and yielded passively to the will of its Creator, though groaning and travailing in pain under the bondage of "him that had the power of death, that is, the devil," (Heb. ii. 14,) "the prince of the power of the air," (Eph. ii. 2.) Its perishing condition the creature would not bemoan, were it still permitted to offer itself up for the preservation and gladness of man, as he was in paradise, created in God's image. But that, as companion in tribulation with God's suffering children, it has to endure violence and injustice from the ungrateful and wicked, that it is ill-treated and tormented by "unjust stewards," and the countless idolaters who pervert the truth of the creature's hope into the lie of their hope in the creature; thereat "the whole creation groaneth and travaileth in pain until now." "Subject to vanity" Paul styles the great tragedy of the creature's present woful existence. Even the service which it gladly yields to man—to the vineyard's grateful dresser and the flock's pious shepherd (1 Cor. ix. 7)—is embittered, because it serves corruption: "Meats for the belly, and the belly for meats; but God shall destroy both it and them," (1 Cor. vi. 13.) That "all is to perish with the using" is the bitter by-taste of death it has received from man's death. "In hope" was the sound in Paul's Christian ear when hearkening to the plaintive melodies pervading all nature. The green trees of the forest are sad that they have to serve idolaters, and they stretch forth their tops in expectation of the days when they shall "clap their hands" for joy over the glory of God's children, (Isa. lv. 12.) The sea reluctantly bears ships with idolatrous signs devoted to Mammon's service, and would fain foam forth her music to the last advent. The whole earth pants under the load of the daily countless acts of injustice and violence committed on her surface, and longs after her change into an "habitation of righteousness." The sun feels impatient to shine down from year to year upon the misdeeds of the wicked. Oh that it might soon lose its shine, after the manner in which it grew pale at Damascus before the heavenly brightness of the Lord! Yea, heaven and earth, both partakers in Zion's captivity, tarry for their redemption, like the weary labourer for the approach of his holiday. But the glorious end of their tarrying is pledged also in Christ, "the firstborn of every creature," (Col. i. 15.) As much as "the second Man, the Lord from heaven," under whose feet God hath put all things, is "worthy of higher honour" than "the first man, of the earth," so much more gloriously also will the creature be adorned, when in the "regeneration" (Matt. xix. 28) it shall stand forth a joyful participator in the final redemption of God's children, in their glorious freedom from Satan, sin, and death, itself freed also from the yoke of corruptible bondage, no longer "unwillingly," but again willingly to serve, in new wise, its legitimate lords. (Cf. Matt. xxvi. 29.) Then the plaintive symphonies of creation's groans shall have an end, and be swallowed up in the redeemed's endless hymns of "hosannah" sung to God. Paul understood the speechless aspirations of creation under the creature's groaning anguish, ("we know" is his expression,) for he found them re-echoed in God's children, who themselves also are made to groan in their mortal bodies, for whose redemption they are waiting: "And not only they, but ourselves also, which have the first-fruits of the Spirit, even we ourselves groan within ourselves, waiting for the adoption, to wit, the redemption of the body."

Is there anything greater than the hope that Paul had in Christ Jesus? "And now abideth faith, hope, charity, these three; but the greatest of these is *charity*." In the light of the epiphany of glory, which in the followers of Christ already manifests itself here on earth, and which shall never cease, let us now view Paul in the next chapter.

> "Zion hears the watchmen singing,
> And all her heart for joy is springing;
> She wakes, she rises from her gloom,
> For her Lord comes down all-glorious,
> Is strong in grace, in truth victorious;
> Her star is risen, her light is come!
> Ah, come, Thou blessed One,
> God's own beloved Son.
> Hallelujah!
> We follow, till the halls we see,
> Where Thou hast bid us sup with Thee."

## IX.

## THE MAN OF LOVE.

*"Be ye followers of me, even as I also am of Christ."*—1 COR. xi. 1.

LOVE is life in others, life of Me in Thee. In Christ was manifested bodily the love that dwells in God, and the disciple whom Jesus loved drank it in at the breast of the Son of man. *Pectus facit theologum,* 'tis the heart makes the divine. St John the divine's sentence is, " Every one that loveth is born of God, and knoweth God. He that loveth not, knoweth not God; for God is love," (1 John iv. 7, 8.) That "the same anointing" teacheth the Christian all things, (1 John ii. 27,) we may see also in Paul, made by the grace of Christ's Spirit "the man of love." Where he extols love, it is at times as if one heard even St John speak. And yet we find here also the man again who once laboured and wearied himself under the law, but has now, in Christ, learned to rejoice in the fulfilment of the law. Having apprehended the righteousness by faith in opposition to that by works, and Christian hope in opposition to that of carnal Judaism, and being thus forced from the bondage of the law, he counts love to be "the law of Christ," (Gal. vi. 2;) and in the very place where he declares that to them that are without law, himself had become as without law, he feels constrained to insert, "Being not without law to God, but under the law of Christ," (1 Cor. ix. 21.) All that rich admonition, wherein he presents himself to his brethren as a free evangelical

Christian, whose love makes him the servant of all, he closes with the sentence we have taken for the heading of this chapter, "Be ye followers of me, even as I also am of Christ."

In Christ Jesus his Lord he has met with "truth" personified, (Eph. iv. 21,) the form of which he found in the law, (Rom. ii. 20.) That Christ be formed in his "little children," as in himself, thereunto he laboured like one "travailing in birth," (Gal. iv. 19;) and this forming of Christ in them is perfected in love. He stirs up the "love of the Spirit" (Rom xv. 30) in the brethren that have the " Spirit of Christ," and therefore are His, (Rom. viii. 9;) the fellowship of the Spirit is shewn in likemindedness, "having the same love, being of one accord, of one mind," (Phil. ii. 1, 2.) To the young Christians at Thessalonica, whom he cherished, "even as a nurse her children," (1 Thess. ii. 7,) he found it not needful to write of "brotherly love," themselves being "taught of God to love one another," (1 Thess. iv. 9;) for where "faith groweth," there "charity aboundeth," (2 Thess. i. 3.) To them who, according to the riches of God's glory, are strengthened with might by His Spirit in the inner man, it is given to have Christ dwelling in their hearts by faith, whereby they are "rooted and grounded in love;" that they may be able to comprehend with all saints the all-abounding "love of Christ, which passeth knowledge," that they may be filled with all the fulness of God, (Eph. iii. 16, 19.) Knowledge without love is naught; but being "knit together in love," Christians will attain "unto all riches of the full assurance of understanding," and of the mystery of Christ, "in whom are hid all the treasures of wisdom and knowledge," (Col. ii. 2, 3.) To the "foolish Galatians," who, in their legalising, were hewing out for themselves " broken cisterns, that can hold no water," (Jer. ii. 13,) and whose love therefore was pining away, he exclaims, "Christ is become of no effect unto you; whosoever of you are justified by the law, ye are fallen from grace. For we through the Spirit wait for the hope of righteousness by faith. For in Jesus Christ neither circumcision availeth anything, nor uncircumcision; but faith which worketh by love," (Gal. v. 4, 6.) Thus also "we establish the law through faith," (Rom. iii. 31;) because faith, having received Christ by grace, lives by and in His love, which is "the fulfilling of the law." What Moses' law is claim-wise, Christ's gospel is gift-wise, viz., the impress of God's holy love; and it is out of the gospel ("by the mercies of God," Rom. xii. 1) that the Apostle draws the courage to exhort his flocks, "Be ye therefore followers of God, as dear children, and walk in love, as Christ also hath loved us, and hath given Himself for us an offering and a sacrifice to God for a sweet-smelling savour," (Eph. v. 1, 2.) "Put on therefore, as the elect of God, holy and beloved, bowels of mercies, kindness, humbleness of mind, meekness, longsuffering, forbearing one another, and forgiving one another; if any man have a quarrel against any, even as Christ forgave you, so also do ye. And above all these things put on charity, which is the bond of perfectness," (Col. iii. 12, 14.) In the admonitory part of his Epistle to the Romans love assumes her highest height. Having attired the saints with the double necklace of "brotherly love" (the holy στοργή, relation-love) and "love to enemies," (chap. xii.,) and exhorted the "heavenly citizens" by well-doing to prove themselves good and conscientious subjects unto the powers that be, he shews them how richly they possess everything needful to prove before the Gentiles, by their honest walk among them, "as in the day," that the gospel-day had indeed set in; and, summing up all in one, he says, "Owe no man anything, but to love one another; for he that loveth another hath fulfilled the law," (chap. xiii. 8.) Everywhere does the "debtor" both to the Greeks and Barbarians (chap. i. 14) shew himself an example of that love, wherein one owes himself to other. His whole life is one continued payment of the debt of love to which the Lord Jesus bound him, when He forgave him all his debt; and because love never ceases, we see in him what Augustine says of love's paying and yet remaining in debt: "Love giveth in paying debts, yet, after giving, always remaineth 'herself' in debt. Time never will be that she is not paying; nor doth she ever lose, but rather multiplieth herself in giving." If it could be said of any man that (in this sense) he paid all he owes, it was Paul, who ever continued in the payment of love's unceasing debt, (Heb. xiii. 1;) for the unanimous claim, the sum and substance of all commandments, is, Thou shalt love. Quite at one with St John, Paul beholds the manifestation of the love of God in brotherly love, (1 John iv. 21,) and gives to this the prize of law's fulfilment, (Rom. xiii. 8.) How had he been so blind aforetime, when fancying to himself that the law could make of him a man of love? But now, without its aid and co-operation, the law found itself fulfilled in the servant and follower of Jesus Christ. The complete fulfiller of all righteousness required by the law is Christ for us, and Christ's Spirit in us. Love, which is its fulfilling, (Rom. xiii. 10,) is ever growing, therefore never perfect in us, but is well-pleasing and acceptable unto God in Christ our intercessor and advocate.

The apostolic declaration, that "he that loveth another hath fulfilled the law," has a twofold import. First, love is that deed required by the law, in which all other deeds required by it are contained and summed up. "For this," he immediately continues, "thou shalt not commit adultery, thou shalt not kill, thou shalt not steal, thou shalt not bear false witness, thou shalt not covet; and if there be any other commandment, it is briefly comprehended in this saying, namely, Thou shalt love thy neighbour as thyself." Therein, then, consists the Christian's freedom from the law, that neither is he driven to any work of the law, through which he has still to become righteous before God, nor is he bound to any but the "new commandment," (John xiii. 34,) which he readily and gladly fulfils—and wherein he accurately hits the eternal sense of all law's commandments—by the spirit of love. Luther, according to the sense given him of Paul's gospel, says, "Thus, then, this commandment of love is a short commandment, and yet a long one; it is but one, and yet many; none, and yet all; one, and short in itself, and soon understood, but long and many in practice, for it comprehends and rules all; it is no commandment in respect to works, for it names none as its own in particular, and yet it contains all, because all are, and must be, its own. Thus the commandment of love annuls all others, and yet establishes them all; and that for this reason, and to this end, that we may learn and know to keep and to esteem no commandment or work other than is required and bidden by love." Where, for instance, the Apostle charges husbands and wives with their duty one toward another, what else does he but enlarge on the commandment of love? "I think also that I have the Spirit of God," he ventures to say, (1 Cor. vii. 40.) But the Spirit of God is love. "Love worketh no ill to his neighbour; therefore love is the fulfilling of the law." "Have love," saith Augustine, in one mind with Paul, "and do what thou wilt." But more still. For Paul also calls love the "fulfilling," or filling up, of the law, because it fills up its empty form with real substance; so that the manifold riches contained in each commandment are made apparent. Works conformable to law, without love, are but empty nutshells. Yea, works the most splendid, such as bestowing all one's goods to feed the poor, and even acts of martyrdom—the giving one's body to be burnt—Paul declares to be without profit if they lack the moving principle, which alone gives and can give them reality, and heart, and soul—viz., love, (1 Cor. xiii. 3.) Out of the seed of Christ's Spirit love grows into, and puts life into, every form and kind of fruit, which God has delineated in His commandments, all commandments of love; and this is the evangelical use of the law, as taught by Paul, that the Christian in his walk of love be led by the light of God's commandments, as by the reins of the spiritual law, by which the law of the Spirit (or of Christ, or of faith) with mild and yet lordly hand guides the children of the Spirit. How finely does the Apostle understand how to draw forth the sense of love from under the veil even of outward ordinances! "It is written in the law of Moses, Thou shalt not muzzle the mouth of the ox that treadeth out the corn. Does God take care for oxen? or saith He it altogether for our sakes?" (1 Cor. ix. 9, 10.)

What Christian heart can help being touched, when, on Palm-Sunday, the Epistle is read of the humiliation and exaltation of our blessed Saviour—an Epistle, the mysterious doctrine of which Paul introduces in these words, "Let this mind be in you which was also in Christ Jesus," (Phil. ii. 5.) That mind of love he means, which will prompt Christ's followers to "do nothing through strife or vainglory, in lowliness of mind each esteeming other better than himself, none looking on his own things, but every man also on the things of others." Wherever he places Christ's example before his own and his brethren's eyes, he beholds love in the foreground, that love which divests herself of her own, condescends to the lowly, and enriches the poor. He will not command the Corinthians into welldoing to their poor brethren at Jerusalem ; but by a graphic depicting of the abundant liberality of the churches in Macedonia, he will prove the sincerity of their love; and then points them to Christ's example of love, as the fundamental motive to all ours : " For ye know the grace of our Lord Jesus Christ, that though He was rich, yet for your sakes He became poor, that ye through His poverty might be rich," (2 Cor. viii. 9.) And of the Romans, for whose faith he fervently thanks God, he demanded—"by the mercies of God"—as their best sacrifice, that of their own selves. " For even Christ," he says, "pleased not Himself;" "wherefore receive ye one another, as Christ also received us to the glory of God," (Rom. xv. 3, 7.) Paul's whole life is perfumed with the sweet savour of self-sacrificing love. We know in what high estimation he held evangelical liberty, and how he burnt in holy zeal against those who would rob others of this inestimable treasure. " Beware of dogs," he could break forth against them, " beware of evil workers, beware of the concision; for we are the circumcision, which worship God in the Spirit, and rejoice in Christ Jesus, and have no confidence in the flesh," (Phil. iii. 2, 3.) But while in his heart "before God" faith reigned supreme, (Rom. xiv. 22,) he yielded to love the supremacy in relation to his neighbour. "Though I be free from all men,—for why is my liberty judged of another man's conscience? (1 Cor. x. 29,)—yet have I made myself servant unto all, that I might gain the more," (1 Cor. ix. 19.) It would have been to him a bringing under the power of something else than Christ, had he felt himself hindered by anything from foregoing, and leaving undone what he, to possess and to do, had the power. He was far from thinking that he had received his gospel liberty, his evangelical knowledge and strength of faith, in order to please himself in them. Nay, with burning sympathy to feel, as his own, the offences of the meanest among his flock, (2 Cor. xi. 29;) with strong shoulders to bear the infirmities of the weak; to sacrifice his power, rather than by the use of it to shew his Christian liberty, where either it might save many, or save offence to a single brother; to turn all to the best, and recognise the scrupulous and narrow-minded as brethren also for whom Christ died, as servants living unto the Lord, standing and falling to their own Master, (Rom. xiv.,)—this was Paul's mind, and therein he walked according to love. The Corinthians had seen what he wrote in 1 Cor. viii.-x.; the more boldly then could he exhort them, "Let no man seek his own, but every one another's wealth," (1 Cor. x. 24;) while the Romans could read Rom. xiv., under the testimony of many witnesses that the Apostle had drawn his own portrait. "*Quod nos docemus, ille vivit*," (what we teach, he lives,) said Luther of Nicolas Hausmann, a Pauline follower of Christ.

Gregory of Nazianzum read in Paul's Epistles what Paul says himself of Paul. The breath of the Spirit of revelation pervades the speech of the holy man of God; wherefore his words are no dead letters, but full of soul, "having hands and feet," as Luther says, because they bring the man Paul to our view as he verily lives and moves in Christ. "For we write none other things unto you than what (plainly told) ye read or acknowledge, and I trust ye shall acknowledge to the end; as also ye have acknowledged us in part, that we are your rejoicing, even as ye also are ours in the day of the Lord Jesus," (2 Cor. i. 13, 14.) It is in this view that we shall now proceed to consider his masterly panegyric upon love ("charity") in 1 Cor. xiii.; and we shall find that, upon the "more excellent way," which here he shews the Corinthians and us all, himself has preceded his brethren as the follower of Christ.

"Though I speak with the tongues of men and of angels, and have not charity, I am become as sounding brass or a tinkling cymbal." Paul thanked God that he spoke with tongues more than all the Corinthians, (1 Cor. xiv. 18;) but though it be in the speech of angels that behold God's face, yet would he be like a clock or cymbal, that gives forth its sound without either feeling or consciousness, unless he be moved by the love which the Spirit of God infuses into that of man. He was conscious, then, that love to God and the Father of our Lord Jesus Christ, love to His people, love to all men, was the moving soul of all his speaking with tongues. God was the witness of his love, whom he served with his spirit in the Gospel of His Son, (Rom. i. 9.) Therefore, though he could speak with tongues more than they all, he strove most, and loved best, to speak God's word so plainly "with the understanding," that the most unlearned who heard him might say "Amen" to it. "In the church I had rather speak five words with my understanding, than ten thousand words in an unknown tongue," (1 Cor. xiv. 19.) He gladly bore to have the "milk" of his apostolic teaching (1 Cor. iii. 2) less valued by the Corinthians, than the malmsey of their speaking in tongues; but he bears down all who think themselves prophets, or spiritual, by this crushing sentence:—"The things that I write unto you are the commandments of the Lord," (1 Cor. xiv. 37;) cutting short those who will not acknowledge church precepts and order as "the commandments of the Lord," by saying: "But if any man be ignorant, let him be ignorant," (1 Cor. v. 38.) But not only was the speaking with tongues valueless in Paul's eye, unless the sounding instrument be tuned by love; but he goes further:—"And though I have the gift of prophecy, and understand all mysteries, and all knowledge; and though I have all faith, so that I could remove mountains, and have not charity, I am nothing." We know him, the man of prophecy, and of knowledge in the mystery of Christ, the preacher of the Gospel; but though his knowledge and prophecy were no more "in part," but already "perfect," after the manner of "seeing face to face," yet would he not be acknowledged by Christ, but be "a cast-away," unless he preached the Gospel out of love to Him and to souls, whom the preached Word is powerful to win and save. It was, therefore, with a shepherd's care and love, with the wisdom of a father and the tenderness of a mother, yea, and the carefulness of a nurse, (1 Thess. ii. 7,) that the Apostle of the Gentiles cared for the sheep and lambs whom he had brought into the fold of Christ. In "labour of love" (1 Thess. i. 3) we have seen the "labourer together with God" (1 Cor. iii. 9) accomplish his course from Corinth to Jerusalem, from Jerusalem to Rome. All his epistles draw forth the treasure of prophecy and doctrine out of a heart filled with holy delight in his flocks. Love taught him not to please himself in writing to them, not to be led away by his own, though spiritual, inclination, but to speak and write always and everywhere to edification, without any unfaithful keeping back of what was profitable unto them, (Acts xx. 20,) whether it please or displease, (Gal. i. 10; 1 Thess. ii. 4, 5;) but also without any unchaste obtrusion of mysteries unprofitable to godliness. "For whether we be beside ourselves, it is to God; or whether we be sober, it is for your cause," he writes to the Corinthians, (2 Cor. v. 13,) to whom his slanderers had probably whispered into the ear that their dry and sober teacher, Paul, lacked that genial flight of enthusiasm to be expected of an apostle. Casual throughout, serving actual wants, and suited to individual circumstances, are all his apostolic epistles, while inspired by the Comforter and dictated by the love of Christ; and

L

exactly so they required all to be written, in order to strike into heart and life—then, now, and at all times. Without love, the preacher Paul had not only himself been unblest, but without that love, which—taught by the Spirit—gave him the measure and wording of wholesome doctrine in all things, the Church of Christ would not have had in him the man, who, as he came to the Romans, comes to us all "in the fulness of the blessing of the Gospel of Christ," (Rom. xv. 29.) How intent he was not to be a mere verbal preacher of the Gospel, but by his life also to shew forth the self-sacrificing love of Christ, we are made to feel by his equally bold and humble words: "It were better for me to die, than that any man should make my glorying void. For though I preach the Gospel, I have nothing to glory of; for necessity is laid upon me; yea, woe is unto me, if I preach not the Gospel!" So effectually had the Lord called him to preach the Gospel, that to shrink from it would have been mortal sin to him. To a voluntary labourer's wages the "unprofitable servant" (Luke xvii. 10) laid no claim. With him it indeed was "life for life." And therefore he felt it his duty in his own person to forego the reward, of which otherwise the labourer in the Gospel is worthy, (Luke x. 7; 1 Thess. v. 18,) and to preach the same "without charge," (1 Cor. ix. 14-18.) But though he "could remove mountains" by faith, to which "nothing shall be impossible," (Matt. xvii. 20,) yet were he "nothing," unless his wonder-working faith (1 Cor. xii. 9) be but the handmaid of love. An apostle's signs truly were wrought among the Corinthians, but before those of "wonders and mighty deeds" he puts love's own sign, that of "patience," (2 Cor. xii. 12.) So, like a true follower of his Master, he humbly refrained from using his gift of working miracles, (1 Cor. xii. 10,) otherwise than in love to others, not to his own pleasing. While

Publius' father and many others were healed by him on the same island, (Acts xxviii. 8, 9,) he writes, in sad yet humble resignation, to Timothy: "But Trophimus have I left at Miletum sick," (2 Tim. iv. 20.) He had been afraid to rob this brother of the blessings of an illness, to please himself by his company, when restored to health. That with him genuine and "full" deeds were only those of love, we have seen in Rom. xiii. "And though I bestow all my goods to feed the poor, and though I give my body to be burned, and have not charity, it profiteth me nothing." Therefore he wished to "seal" to the church at Jerusalem the "fruit" of the love of her daughter churches by his testimony of its genuineness, (Rom. xv. 28,)—viz., that it was a "fruit of their righteousness," (2 Cor. ix. 10.) This may also throw light upon the persecuted Apostle's flight from city to city. Love rendered him as capable of escaping the crown of martyrdom, though he had to be let "through a window in a basket," (2 Cor. xi. 33,) as it made him ready to suffer all things for the Gospel's sake and its confessors.

And now (from ver. 4) Paul conducts us into a garden of love, where bed upon bed stands furnished with heavenly plants. His own heart was such a garden of love. "Into thy heart," says Gregory the Great, "must thou dip the pen that shall write the truth legibly into others' hearts." This did Paul. "Charity suffereth long and is kind." Paul was no stranger to Adam's common legacy, selfishness; nay, his own was rather sharply developed in a naturally harsh temper of choleric rashness. But, lo, what hath grace made of him! How lovely does the double flower of long-suffering and kindness exhale her sweet fragrance in this man of God! The follower of Him he has become, in whom Matthew sees Isaiah's word fulfilled, (Isa. xlii. 2, 3.) "He shall not strive, nor cry;

neither shall any man hear His voice in the streets. A bruised reed shall He not break, and smoking flax shall He not quench," (Matt. xii. 19, 20.) In "beseeching" and "praying" lay the power of this "ambassador for Christ," (2 Cor. v. 20.) It was "by long-suffering and kindness, by the Holy Ghost and love unfeigned," that this "soldier of Christ" so successfully wielded the weapons of his warfare, (2 Cor. vi. 6.) Had he to rebuke? he would rather than "with a rod" do so "in love, and in the spirit of meekness," (1 Cor. iv. 21.) Was he grieved over their "divisions?" he would "beseech" them as "brethren," (1 Cor. i. 10;) always, and first of all, thanking God on their behalf for the grace of God given them by Jesus Christ, (ib. ver. 4.) When speaking to children who demeaned themselves, as if they could sit in judgment over their "weak," "despised," "persecuted," and everywhere "buffeted" fathers, he could indeed give expression to his emotion in words which must have been felt by them like spears and lances, as in 1 Cor. iv. 8, &c. "Now ye are full, now ye are rich, ye have reigned as kings without us; and I would to God ye did reign, [viz., as Christians shall reign with Christ,] that we also might reign with you. We are fools for Christ's sake, but ye are wise in Christ, [know how to adorn with wise words the foolish word of the Cross:] we are weak, but ye are strong: ye are honourable, but we are despised." But what makes him write so? It was the genuine earnestness of love. "I write not these things to shame you, but as my beloved sons I warn you." Might some, against whom he was "bold," even think of him, as if he "walked according to the flesh?" (2 Cor. x. 2,) before God he was manifest in the love of the Spirit. Full of tender forbearance, he opens his Second Epistle to the Corinthians by relating to that congregation, which had caused him so much grief, all his sufferings, comforting himself by their prayers for him, (2 Cor. i. 11.) "Let the righteous smite me; it shall be a kindness; and let him reprove me; it shall be an excellent oil, which shall not break my head: for yet my prayer also shall be in their calamities," (Ps. cxli. 5.) These words of the man after God's heart found their counterpart here, and were acted over again between Paul and the Corinthians; for friendlier reproved than they were by him could no 'one be. To their love he appeals, even he whom they had deeply grieved by the want of it; "having confidence," he says, "in you all, that my joy is the joy of you all," (2 Cor. ii. 3.) With what lovely tenderness does he write: "If any" (he forbears to name the incestuous person) "have caused grief, he hath not grieved me, but in part; that I may not overcharge you all, [with him.] Sufficient to such a man is this punishment, which was inflicted of many. So that contrariwise ye ought rather to forgive him, and comfort him, lest perhaps such an one should be swallowed up with overmuch sorrow. Wherefore I beseech you, that ye would confirm your love toward him," (2 Cor. ii. 5-8.) Yea, that he had to afflict his beloved Corinthians by a punitive epistle, even them who indeed should have made him glad, and in whom he ought rather to have rejoiced, (2 Cor. ii. 2, 3,) this went so to his heart, that he had already repented of it; but now he rejoiced and thanked God for it, seeing that, through His grace, it had wrought in them a "godly sorrow," so that they might receive damage by him in nothing. (2 Cor. vii. 8, 9.) Where he draws the picture of an honest servant of God, he exclaims: "O ye Corinthians, our mouth is open unto you, our heart is enlarged. Ye are not straitened in us, but ye are straitened in your own bowels. Now, for a recompence in the same, (I speak as unto my children,) be ye also enlarged," (2 Cor. vi. 11-13.) Finally, after the whole earnestness and holy zeal of an apostle had, like a heavy thunder-cloud, discharged itself over the heads of the Corinthians, or rather their disturbers, there breaks through the scattered clouds, like the sun in its noontide brightness, all the kindness and gentleness of love: "Finally, brethren, farewell, [literally, rejoice.] Be perfect, be of good comfort, be of one mind, live in peace; and the God of love and peace shall be with you," (2 Cor. xiii. 11.) Such was their apostle! a beseecher "by the meekness and gentleness of Christ," (2 Cor. x. 1.) Truly this Second Epistle to the Corinthians is itself a commentary throughout on that passage, "We persuade men: but are made manifest unto God," (2 Cor. v. 11.) "Without dissimulation" indeed was the Apostle's love, and unmixed with any effeminacy; decided his break with evil—he abhorred it; firm his love of good—he clave unto it, (Rom. xii. 9.) Hardened sinners he "delivered unto Satan," (1 Cor. v. 5; 1 Tim. i. 20;) yet bore them but the more fervently upon his heart to the saving of their spirit, (cf. 2 Cor. ii. 5-11,) and charged Timothy to do the same, (2 Tim. ii. 25, 26.) "O foolish Galatians," he exclaims, with energetic indignation, "who hath bewitched you, that ye should not obey the truth?" (Gal. iii. 1.) Yet how affectionately does he "beseech" them not to be snared into bondage again unto the "weak and beggarly elements." "Brethren," he says, "be as I am; for I am as ye are," (Gal. iv. 12.) And not to shame them before a third person, he wrote to them, against his custom, with his "own hand," a "large letter," literally, *in large letters*, that they might not need a reader, thus seeking to please them, (Gal. vi. 11.) The same desire is touchingly evidenced by his postscript "token in every epistle" which he wrote by dictation, (2 Thess. iii. 17.) Sometimes, as he takes up the pen to write "the salutation by me Paul with mine own hand," (1 Cor. xvi. 22,) he is moved with indignation when he thinks of the false brethren among those he addresses, and adds, "If any man love not the Lord Jesus Christ, let him be Anathema, Maran-atha," ere he continues, "The grace of our Lord Jesus Christ be with you. My love be with you all in Christ Jesus." At other times he will feel his hand cramped by the fetters which bind him to the soldier who guards him, (Acts xxviii. 16, 20,) and adds to "the salutation by the hand of me Paul,"—"Remember my bonds," (Col. iv. 18.) But he always ends by wishing them "grace," to which at times he adds a few last words of affectionate remembrance, such as, "My love be with you all in Christ Jesus."\* In the kindliness of his friendship he does not think it too mean to watch with a mother's tender care over the health of his young son Timothy: "Drink no longer water, but use a little wine for thy stomach's sake, and thine often infirmities," (1 Tim. v. 23.) With all his freedom in Christ to *enjoin* Philemon that which is convenient, he will rather *beseech* him for love's sake, (Philem. viii. 9.) The Philippians' care and liberality he acknowledges in a manner that makes one feel that he rejoices in the soul of the givers, and accepts for their joy what they so gladly give, (Phil. iv. 10, &c.) And now, one glance still upon that salutation chapter, Rom. xvi. It is full of gentle and affectionate love. First he commends Phœbe, the bearer of the epistle, as his kind "succourer," to the love of the Roman church. Next he greets Priscilla and Aquila, and remembers with fervent gratitude their services in the Lord to all the churches of the Gentiles. In the remembrance of his love lives Epænetus beside Stephanas, as the "first-

\* Cf. the introduction to the instructive work "The Life and Epistles of St Paul," by W. J. Conybeare and J. S. Howson. London. 1853. Vol. I., p. xii.

fruits of Achaia," (1 Cor. xvi. 5.) Mary's much labour bestowed on him he cannot forget; neither what Andronicus and Junia, his kinsmen and fellow-prisoners have been to him before he was in Christ.* All are "his beloved," yet only three of them he greets expressly with this epithet, probably because they most needed his assurance of it. Of Amplias, he says specially that he was worthy of his love "in the Lord." With Apelles "approved in Christ" he joins them of Aristobulus' household, and with his kinsman Herodion them of Narcissus' household—with poor domestics the free, who were one with them in the Lord. Tryphena and Tryphosa, two female labourers, he greets before; but trusts to their modesty that they will gladly join him in saying, that she hath "laboured *much* in the Lord." And how tenderly does he express his love in saluting "Rufus, chosen in the Lord, and his mother and mine." Lastly, he salutes two pairs, each of five, with evident pleasure in their communion, and lets them know to their surprise that their names obscure in the world are remembered and borne in his heart. "With an holy kiss" he seals these thirty salutations. In this kindly manner did the man upon whom came daily "the care of all the churches," (2 Cor. xi. 28,) which lay scattered over east and west, bear the single souls of them individually upon his heart, with love's affectionate remembrance.

"Charity envieth not." Might Apollos be preferred to him by the fastidious Corinthians? Paul grudged him not that gift of eloquence himself lacked, nor thought for a moment of suspecting his fellow-servant in the Lord to have had any share in the Corinthians' strife and divisions,

---

* Here the author supposes Paul to have borne his kinsmen's *prayers* for him, before he was in Christ, in grateful remembrance, and does not mean to insinuate that they had been at all *directly* instrumental in his conversion, which the peculiar and sudden manner of it forbids us to think.—Tr.

(cf. 1 Cor. iii. and iv. 6.) Yea, so far was he from any feeling of jealousy, that he did all he could to prevail on Apollos to return to Corinth, (1 Cor. xvi. 12.) When he learnt at Rome that some were preaching Christ even of envy and strife, "supposing"—*i.e.*, wishing by their contention—"to add affliction to his bonds," and thus eventually to see him shut out from all the honour of evangelical preaching, he was so free from ignoble envy, that he could write : "What then? notwithstanding, every way, whether in pretence, or in truth, Christ is preached; and I therein do rejoice, yea, and will rejoice, (Phil. i. 15-18.) An envious Paul, how absurd it sounds! No, the man who has transmitted to us the Lord's saying, "It is more blessed to give than to receive," (Acts xx. 35,) and who so richly tasted the blessedness of giving, could suffer no "rottenness in his bones," (Prov. xiv. 30.)

"Charity vaunteth not itself, is not puffed up, doth not behave itself unseemly." This tricolor also belongs to Paul's heraldry of love. A pert and saucy boy, (who, it should seem, was as well acquainted with the rod—cf. Heb. xii. 9—as poor little Martin,*) and a bold, forward youth Saul doubtless was. A rash temper, haughty demeanour, and obstinate, dogmatical spirit, we may, without fear of slander, ascribe to his unsubdued and determined nature. And now, in how different a light does the character of "the man of love" stand before us, even in the smallest matters! Did the obstinacy of his old Adam once shew itself in the sharp contention he had with Barnabas about Mark? (Acts. xv. 37-39,) this only proves how tightly otherwise he held his flesh in reins by the spirit. Most lovely does this reining in, the moderation, or let me call it the holy collectedness of the man of love, appear in his character as shepherd tending the weak among his flock;

* Luther.

in which character he was best known to the Corinthians: "For though ye have ten thousand instructors in Christ, yet have ye not many fathers; for in Christ Jesus I have begotten you through the Gospel. Wherefore I beseech you, be ye followers of me," (1 Cor. iv. 15, 16.) He had the shepherd's heart and kindly care of a Jacob: "My Lord knoweth that the children are tender, and the flocks and herds with young are with me; and if men should overdrive them one day, all the flock will die," (Gen. xxxiii. 13.) The parable of the imperceptibly-growing seed, (Mark iv. 26-29,) this the labourer in God's husbandry had apprehended with the sense of love, and he acted accordingly. The unfeigned humility of this high Apostle is the best comment on the word "charity vaunteth not itself, is not puffed up." As oft as he addresses his flocks—Christ's flocks—as "brethren," he includes himself as their fellow-sinner, and partaker with them of the same grace of Jesus Christ. When longing to impart to the Romans some spiritual gift to the end they may be established, he at once adds: "That is, that I may be comforted together with you by the mutual faith both of you and me," (Rom. i. 11, 12;) yea, he almost apologises for his boldness in writing to them: "And I myself also am persuaded of you, my brethren, that ye also are full of goodness, filled with all knowledge, able also to admonish one another. Nevertheless, brethren, I have written the more boldly unto you in some sort, as putting you in mind, because of the grace that is given to me of God," (Rom. xv. 14, 15.) Thus he entirely subjected his own gift of grace to preach the Word under the grace of the Word itself, and set himself the example to his brethren in walking after the rule, that no man should think of himself more highly than he ought to think, but to think soberly, according as God hath dealt to every man the measure of faith, (Rom. xii. 3,) "Who then is Paul?" he asks, jealous for God's honour, "and who is Apollos, but ministers by whom ye believed, even as the Lord gave to every man? I have planted, Apollos watered, but God gave the increase. So then neither is he that planteth anything, neither he that watereth; but God that giveth the increase," (1 Cor. iii. 5-7.) "Charity is not puffed up," might especially remind the Corinthians, inflated with the conceit of their knowledge, of what Paul had before said: "Knowledge puffeth up, but charity edifieth," (1 Cor. viii. 1.) Who possessed the gift of knowledge more then he? But he would have the weak and less-gifted brethren to be undespised, and everywhere he used the power which the Lord had given him "to edification, and not to destruction," (2 Cor. x. 8, xiii. 10.) The third property of love also—its good grace and proper tact, which leads it not to behave itself unseemly—is finely stamped in Paul's character. Sober and honest, just and true, gracious and edifying, pure and lovely is the Christian walk in love to which he so often exhorts, (Rom. xii. 17, xiii. 13; Eph. iv. 29; Phil. iv. 8,) and wherein he sets the example. A gracious and noble demeanour is perhaps the most prominent feature in his conduct towards all men. We may here be reminded of the magistrates at Philippi—the chiefs of Asia at Ephesus —the chief captain, Claudius Lysias—the two governors, Felix and Festus—King Agrippa and Julius the Roman centurion,—all of whom were forced to admire the courteous frankness, decorum and propriety of the "prisoner" of the Lord. Neither did his brotherly love behave itself unseemly. He was far from thinking that the intimacy and close communion of brethren in Christ at all exempt them from due attention to proper deportment, and all that is becoming in the various relations of life. He warns servants not to despise their "believing masters," under the pretence that "they are brethren," (1 Tim. vi. 2;) and with the exhortation to "be kindly affectioned one to another with brotherly love," he couples that of "in honour preferring one another," (Rom. xii. 10.) With his sense of laudable Christian order he deemed it essential to have a brother co-ordinated with him for the conveyance of the churches' gift to Jerusalem. Well might he have claimed their unconditional confidence, but he rather chose the lowlier and more regardful way, as thereby "avoiding this, that no man should blame us in this abundance which is administered by us: providing for honest things, [*i. e.*, having regard to fair dealing,] not only in the sight of the Lord, but also in the sight of men," (2 Cor. viii. 19-21.)

Charity "seeketh not her own,"—not *her* pleasure, not *her* reward, not *her* honour, not *her* liberty, yea, we dare add, not *her* salvation; for altogether she does not seek her own advantage, but that of others,—"love is life in others." This heavenly flower—disinterestedness—is the queen in the garden of love, and all others emit their sweet odours perfumed by hers. Therefore we should have to tell the life of Paul over again, as that of a man in Christ, would we rightly estimate his disinterested, self-sacrificing love. The Corinthians indeed, in reading these words, "charity seeketh not her own," must have seen the man of love stand bodily before their eyes, the man who could write to them,—them who had, alas! sought their own in relation with him, their truest friend. "Receive us; we have wronged no man, we have corrupted no man, we have defrauded no man"—here his affectionate heart checks, and at once impels him to mitigate the gentle reproach implied in this self-defence, by immediately adding: " I speak not this to condemn you, for I have said before, that ye are in our hearts" (he includes Timothy and Titus) " to die and live with you. Great is my boldness of speech toward you, great is my glorying of you : I am filled with comfort, I am exceeding joyful in all our tribulation," (2 Cor. vii. 2-4.) And what was it that thus filled him with comfort, and made him so exceeding joyful, even in all his tribulation? It was the Corinthians' godly sorrow, and their repentance to salvation, (ib. ver. 9, 10.) For what else did he seek by them but the salvation of their souls? "I seek not yours, but you," he says; "for the children ought not to lay up for the parents, but the parents for the children. And I will do more than that—very gladly spend and be spent for you; though the more abundantly I love you, the less I be loved." With cutting irony he gives them to understand that in one thing only he had treated them "inferior to other churches"—viz., in the letting them feel the disinterestedness of his love; "forgive me this wrong." And then, with that humour in which he is fond at times to clothe his most solemn earnest, (Luther resembles him in this,) he prevents their reply by saying, "But be it so, I did not burden you; nevertheless, being crafty, I caught you with guile." Forthwith, however, he assumes his usual seriousness, and adds, in deep earnest, "We speak before God in Christ; but we do all things, dearly beloved, for your edifying," (2 Cor. xii. 13-19.) Neither there sought Paul his own, where, by "glorying" in the abundance of his labours and sufferings, he seeks to wring from the Corinthians the acknowledgment of his apostolical dignity; yea, hardly anywhere has he exercised greater self-denial than when compelled, by those of whom he ought to have been commended, to "become a fool in glorying," (2 Cor. xii. 11.) Luther once drolly said, "I must be my own cuckoo." How mortifying that to the selfish, vainglorious Adam! Or did Paul indeed seek his own in the greatest glory of his life—to stake and forsake all for the work of

Christ, to win souls for Him? Did he misuse the name of Christ for vainglory? "I trust that ye shall know that we are not reprobates," (unapproved,) he writes to the Corinthians, (2 Cor. xiii. 6,) and adds, "Now I pray to God that ye do no evil; not that we should appear approved, but that ye should do that which is honest, though we be as reprobates," (without occasion to prove our approvedness by the exercise of apostolical discipline.) In the place where he expresses his deep satisfaction at the Philippians "holding forth the word of life, that I may rejoice in the day of Christ, that I have not run in vain, neither laboured in vain" and assures them of his readiness to "be offered" with joy "upon the sacrifice and service of their faith,"—there his mind is so purely bent upon the honour of Christ, and the salvation of his brethren, that he commends Timothy to them in these words: "For I have no man like-minded, who will naturally care for your state. For all seek their own, not the things which are Jesus Christ's," (Phil. ii. 16-21.) How he exhorted himself with that exhortation, "Rejoice with them that do rejoice, and weep with them that weep," (Rom. xii. 15,) has often been noted in our sketch. "Who is weak, and I am not weak? who is offended, and I burn not?" (2 Cor. xi. 29.) Love taught him to lose himself in others, and to suppress his sorrow in participation of their welfare and joy. When at Rome he heard of the Philippians' deep sympathy with Epaphroditus, who had been "sick nigh unto death," he deemed it "necessary" speedily to send him to them, "that, when ye see him again, ye may rejoice, and that I may be the less sorrowful," (Phil. ii. 25-28.) Still stronger than we have before heard him declare to the Corinthians his readiness to be offered a sacrifice for their faith, he expresses himself in Rom. ix. 3, a passage which can only be understood by taking his love to be a reflection of Christ's own.

"I could wish," he says, "that myself were accursed from Christ for my brethren, my kinsmen according to the flesh." If it were possible to be accursed from Christ without being wicked, Paul could wish to forego the enjoyment of Christ's blessed presence, and his peace and joy in Him, for the sake of his unhappy brethren. Charity seeketh not her own.

"Is not easily provoked, thinketh no evil; rejoiceth not in iniquity, but rejoiceth in the truth." Who—next after Christ—was ever fed with gall as Paul was? But that his was a love not easily provoked is not shewn only by the word just quoted, and "the truth" of which "*in Christ*" —as well knowing what therewith he was saying—he called upon the Holy Ghost to witness, (Rom. ix. 1;) but his whole walk, from the day of his conversion to his arrival at Rome, as St Luke has spread it before us in "The Acts," is one chain of unprovoked and indestructible love to even his bitterest enemies, the unbelieving Jews. We have edified ourselves by it, when considering Paul, "the labourer," in his gleaning of the Jewish vineyard; and no less in Paul, "the prisoner of Jesus Christ," bound for the hope of Israel. I have read of a Christian who had brought his violent, choleric temper so completely into subjection to the spirit of meekness, that at no affront would he move a muscle of his face, but a gentle smile about *his mouth* would indicate that he was occupied in burying himself with Jesus. In Paul we see this heroism of love to a degree which it might list angels to behold, to the praise of Jesus Christ, whose follower he was. Not by unbelieving Jews and "false brethren" only, but also by ungrateful children and unfaithful friends was his love put to the test; and Satan, doubtless, would often enough stir up the old Adam to flatter the meek Apostle into a "thinking of evil," a bearing in mind, if not resenting, of some experienced injury. Moses, by the Holy Ghost, gives himself this testimony: "Now the man Moses was very meek, above all the men which were upon the face of the earth," (Num. xii. 3.) In Paul's life are similar traces. In highest objectivity he could write of himself: "Ye are witnesses, and God also, how holily, and justly, and unblameably, we behaved ourselves among you that believe," (1 Thess. ii. 10.) But as Moses broke the tables in "hot waxed anger," and could both smite and intercede for his people at the same time, (cf. Exod. xxxii. 19, &c.,) so Paul also gave "place unto wrath," (Rom. xii. 19,) be it by imprecation over the wicked: "The Lord reward him according to his works;" or by deprecation, in behalf of weak and cross-shy disciples: "I pray God that it may not be laid to their charge," (2 Tim. iv. 14, 16.) A reflection of Stephen's face, which once he saw as that of an angel, now rested upon his own, softened by the love of Christ. It had indeed been but human, had he felt a certain 'satisfaction in the misfortunes of the perverse Jews; but he had drunk of Divine love, that rejoiceth not in iniquity, (injustice and wrong,) even where this is meted out to the wicked by instruments ordained for it. Therefore we find him still at Rome, guarding himself against the suspicion, as if he had aught to accuse his nation of, (Rom. xxviii. 19.) Alas! she was accused enough; and Paul, with a true patriot's pang, already saw the Roman eagles gather to their vengeful repast. Paul's love was drawn from that of Christ, who, "when He beheld the city, wept over it," (Luke xix. 41.) "But rejoiceth in the truth;" yea, at the victory of truth the heart of the man of love beats with very joy. In the joy of a holy love to the Church, we have seen him do his work and labour of love; and joy together with them in the truth, was the signature of his Christian and apostolic life. As St John "the elder" had no greater joy than to find his children walk in truth, (2 John iv.,) so likewise Paul, the founder and chief pastor of many churches, and the "helper" of their joy in all, (2 Cor. i. 24.) His whole heart leaps with joy when he beholds the grace and truth of the Gospel in the blessed churches of his planting. "Therefore, my brethren, dearly beloved and longed for, my joy and crown, so stand fast in the Lord, my dearly beloved," (Phil. iv. 1.) "Now we live, if ye stand fast in the Lord. For what thanks can we render to God again for you, for all the joy wherewith we joy for your sakes before our God?" (1 Thess. iii. 8, 9.) Nearly all his letters he begins with gladsome thanks to God; yea, an unceasing thank-offering must have ascended to heaven in the prayers and intercessions of this indefatigable servant of Christ,—" I thank my God upon every remembrance of you, always in every prayer of mine for you all, making request with joy, for your fellowship in the gospel from the first day until now," (Phil. i. 3-5.) His patient love would care to see the least beginnings in Christian life fostered in the "weak" and "feeble-minded," yea, and the "unruly" also; in short, all the new and weak converts he would have the brethren at Thessalonica bear with patience, (1 Thess. v. 14.) For wherever a congregation was gathered in Christ around His gospel, there he beheld "the rivers of water" flow, and trees both great and small, planted by the side of them, grow up to the praise of the Lord, bringing forth their fruit in their season, (Ps. i. 3.) His highest joy, and the one which nearest resembled that of the Good Shepherd himself, we see the loving pastor evince on the return of some stray sheep to the fold. Five times he expresses his joy over the godly sorrowful in that precious chapter, 2 Cor. vii. Like wave upon wave, it rushes along from his overflowing heart in the fourth verse,—" Great is my boldness of

M

speech toward you, great is my glorying of you: I am filled with comfort, I am exceeding joyful in all our tribulation." With that love which "rejoiceth in the truth" did he bear the individual souls of his numerous congregations in his heart. "I have you in my heart," he says to his beloved Philippians, (chap. i. 7;) and to the Corinthians in the chapter just referred to, (ver. 3,) "Ye are in our hearts to die and live with you." Every progress, every important turning-point in his labours, he communicates to them, while his love believes that his joy is theirs also; as, on the other hand, whatever happened to them, both in good days and evil, found in him always a ready echo, either of inmost joy or heartfelt sympathy,—"Whether one member suffer, all the members suffer with it; or one member be honoured, all the members rejoice with it," (1 Cor. xii. 26.) Such is the Church of Christ, and such was Paul her member—a true "Churchman," whose life was organic with hers. But this will be the subject for another—the last—chapter.

Now for love's fourfold triumph sung by Paul:—She "beareth all things, believeth all things, hopeth all things, endureth all things." Love is unconquerable. "Set me as a seal upon thine heart, as a seal upon thine arm: for love is strong as death," (Cant. viii. 6.) What shall quench her flame? Loads of trouble? she beareth all things. Distrust and suspicion? she believeth all things. The headstrong and maliciously perverse? she hopeth all things. The enmity and persecution of the wicked? she endureth all things. Beloved reader, thou hast found in this sketch many traits already of this fourfold conquerous love in Paul's soul. Yet grudge not the pains of looking at the man of love once more, as in the garden of love he stands clad in the "arms" of these four flower-de-luces. Had the Galatians exhausted his painstaking and pains-bearing love? Well might he, with "the marks of the Lord Jesus in his body," demand of them henceforth to trouble him no more. Yet, that he held them firm in love's embrace, willing to cover with the mantle of love all their follies and declensions, if they would but man their souls to a return to Christ, they could plainly read between the lines of even his sharpest reproof,—" I desire to be present with you now, and to change my voice; for I stand in doubt of you," (Gal. iv. 20.) He longed to be present, and to speak with them, like a mother, in tender love, upbraiding her naughty children. In the last word still of this epistle of sorrow, he unfolds his love that beareth all things, and will not quit her hold of a single soul,—"Brethren, the grace of our Lord Jesus Christ be with your spirit. Amen." Or did his faith in the Corinthians give way because there were heretics among them, that had well-nigh succeeded in estranging from him and Christ's Gospel this beloved flock, the seal of his apostleship? (1 Cor. ix. 1, &c.) "There must be heresies among you," he writes, "that they which are approved may be made manifest among you," (1 Cor. xi. 19.) In both epistles to them that inventive love, which seeks to turn everything to the best, and therefore beareth and believeth all things, shines through every page. With an ingenuity and delicacy which only love inspires, he catches at every chord of their heart,—" I speak as to wise men; judge ye what I say," (1 Cor. x. 15; cf. xi. 2,)—in order to draw them out of the entanglements of falsehood to integrity and uprightness; and boldly he believes that the fire of the last day, though it will consume every carnal superstructure reared by them, yet shall spare the believers' own lives, if built on Jesus Christ, the only foundation, (1 Cor. iii. 11-15.) His hope of them is steadfast, (2 Cor. i. 7,) and he rejoices that he has confidence in them in all things,

(2 Cor. vii. 16.) Or did the Jews mock his hope for them away from his heart? He indeed mourns with David that their full table of grace is made a snare unto them "alway" (Rom. xi. 9, 10;) yet he will not permit this to wrest from him his heart's desire and prayer to God that they may be saved, (Rom. x. 1.) And though "blindness in part hath happened to Israel," yet his love is bold enough to hope for God's "mercy upon all," (Rom. xi. 31, 32.) Or, lastly, did he faint or grow impatient under the trials of unceasing persecutions; and the more, when even " all they in Asia turned away" from him? (2 Tim. i. 15.) Nay, in face of his martyrdom, he puts Timothy in mind of his "doctrine, manner of life, purpose, faith, long-suffering, charity, patience," under all "persecutions" and "afflictions," which came unto him "at Antioch, at Iconium, at Lystra;" adding,—"but what persecutions I endured, out of them all the Lord delivered me," (2 Tim. iii. 10, 11.) And, finally, to stir up the same hope and patient love in his beloved son, that made him endure them, he charges him to "remember that Jesus Christ, of the seed of David, was raised from the dead, according to my gospel: wherein I suffer trouble as an evil-doer, even unto bonds; but the word of God is not bound. Therefore I endure all things for the elect's sakes, that they may also obtain the salvation which is in Christ Jesus with eternal glory," (2 Tim. ii. 8-10.)

Nor could such love fail to beget love. Paul certainly was also loved again of many. St Luke, who best understood and loved him, remained faithful to him to the very last, (2 Tim. iv. 11.) With unswerving devotion, too, did Silas justify his confidence in him; and with unflinching fidelity and filial trust did Timothy and Titus remain attached to him. Aquila and Priscilla, Jason, Aristarchus, Epaphroditus, Clement, with many others his fellow-labourers, "whose names"—like that of his Philippian "true yoke-fellow"—"are in the book of life," (Phil. iv. 3,) loved him more than their own lives; Epaphras, Tychicus, and many others, also were his "fellow-servants in the Lord," (cf. Col. iv. 7, &c.) In nearly all his epistles he speaks with fond and grateful remembrance of brethren that love him in the faith, (Tit. iii. 15.) "Comfort," "refresh," "rejoice," and "fill with joy," are his fond expressions when speaking of the love of his brethren. Therefore we find him in all epistles, from first to last, filled with "great desire to see the face" of those that loved him, (Phil. i. 8; 1 Thess. ii. 17; 2 Tim. i. 4, iv. 9.) Yea, the love of his children in Christ was his continual feast, and a foretaste of his heavenly joy. Think of his departure from Miletus! The Ephesians' prayers and tears, the blessings and salutations of peace of all his congregations, accompanied him wherever he went. Their "much" love well-nigh broke his heart. Oh, he was suceptible of love! "As an angel of God, even as Christ Jesus, ye received me," he recalls with sad remembrance to the memory of the Galatians. "Where is then the blessedness ye spake of? for I bear you record, that, if it had been possible, ye would have plucked out your eyes and have given them to me," (Gal. iv. 14, 15.) But because to give is more blessed than to receive, he was indeed more blessed in the love he felt than in that he inspired.

Together with his assurance of salvation by faith, and the joy of his heirship in hope, Paul possessed the glory of love, which goes forth unchanged unto eternal joys, because she is heavenly life already on earth. "Charity never faileth." When prophecies shall "fail," through their final accomplishment; when tongues shall "cease," in the harmonious language of all inhabitants of the New Jerusalem;

when knowledge which is in part shall "vanish away," in that which is perfect,—even then charity shall not fail; she will be the light of joy in the eye of knowledge, the sweetly moved heart in the voice of heavenly tongues. She will then be manifested in her unchangeable Divine nature; freed from all stains of the flesh, and every haze of sin, she will shine forth in spotless lustre and imperishable beauty. He that sits on the throne of glory, Jesus Christ, is all love. Irradiated by His, that of the redeemed will blaze in effulgent transparency; our great Prototype's will be imaged in theirs, and all rays centre in one luminous picture of love. The "beloved of God" are loved with an eternal love, for "their names are written in the book of life," in the heart of God and of the Lamb, the First-born among many brethren, who unceasingly exercises in the heavenly sanctuary the work of perfect brotherly love. There we shall also meet our Paul, to love him for ever. The unity of the Church there and here—this militant, that triumphant; of those walking still by faith in hope, and those living in visible glory—has its seal and pledge in the spirit of love, which never faileth. "And now abideth faith, hope, charity, these three; but the greatest of these is charity." Augustine says in his "Soliloquies:"—"How should faith still have place, where the things believed in are seen? how hope, where the things hoped for are possessed? Love, however, shall not only lose naught, but enter into her own fulness; for even in beholding yonder the only true and real Beauty, she will remain what she is, and increase her being; yea, if she kept not unceasingly her eye open to the highest delight, she could not remain in her most blessed vision." "Be ye followers of me, as I also am of Christ," is Paul's word to the Church, and to us all. So help us God! Amen.

## THE MAN OF LOVE.

Come, thou Spirit of pure Love,
Who dost forth from God proceed;
Never from my heart remove,
Let me all thy impulse heed.
All that seeks self-profit first,
Rather than another's good—
Whether foe or link'd in blood—
Let me hold with Paul accurst;
And my heart henceforward be
Only ruled, O Love, by thee!

## X.

## THE MAN OF THE CHURCH.

"That thou mayest know how thou oughtest to behave thyself in the house of God, which is the church of the living God, the pillar and ground of the truth."—1 TIM. iii. 15.

IT is remarkable that the false witnesses accusing Jesus before the council brought forth just this accusation,—"We have heard Him say, I will destroy this temple that is made with hands, and within three days I will build another made without hands," (Mark xiv. 58.) It shews us that the holy enigma, written over the portal of Christ's public entry upon His prophetic office, (John ii. 19,) had stung the carnal Jews to their very heart, and ever remained a thorn in their eyes. His first confessing martyr, Stephen, saw the same bitter, Temple-proud spirit of the Pharisees rise against him, as he bore witness for the true "house of God" —the Church of Christ. And here is the point where the grace of Jesus Christ met Paul, to reveal before his unveiled eyes the glorious character of Christ's Church, and to make that man of him whose Christian excellence is summed up in calling him "the man of the Church." No sooner had he known Jesus Christ, the crucified and risen Saviour, than it was all over with his knowing any man—yea, were it even the man Christ—after the flesh, (2 Cor. v. 16.) Before the temple of the body of Christ he saw Zion's temple of stone grow pale. Nevertheless, the Old Testament house of God, the honour of which Stephen had surely left untouched, had become no lie with Paul, but, contrariwise, a reality in Christ. There "the shadow of good things to come," which the coming Christ cast before Him into Israel, the people of promise; here the substance of the "good things" themselves in Christ, (Col. ii. 17; Heb. viii. 5, x. 1.) Therefore the New Testament Church was to him the unveiled Israel, receiving into her bosom the fulness of the Gentiles, (Rom. xi. 25, 26,) "the Israel of God," (Gal. vi. 16,) the replenished or fully realised "congregation of the Lord"—to wit, the New Testament *Ecclesia* is synonymous with the Old Testament *Rahal*—which has the Lord for her inheritance, and is again, on her part, the Lord's inheritance. As such Paul constantly views the Church of Christ, both in contrast with the carnal Israel, (1 Cor. x. 16-18,) and as the people of the Spirit, come into the inheritance of the holy people of Israel, (Eph. i. 10, 11.) "The ends of the world" (1 Cor. x. 11) are come upon them that are of the faith of Israel; and it was by losing himself in these "ends" that the Apostle found all his thoughts so richly redound to the praise of the Triune God and His "unspeakable gift," (2 Cor. ix. 15.)

"Saul, Saul, why persecutest thou me?" It was from this "*me*" that Paul took the key which opened to him the "great mystery concerning Christ and the Church," (Eph. v. 32.) In Christ dwelleth "all fulness," (Col. i. 19,) and what was by figure intrusted to the people of Israel, among whom God dwelt, (2 Cor. vi. 16,) that is in full grace and truth imparted to the Church of Christ, "which is His body, the fulness of Him that filleth all in all," (Eph. i. 23.) All things in heaven and earth have been created by Him and for Him, (Col. i. 16,) and He filleth all things with the breath of His glorious power; and therefore needeth indeed no one for the consummation of His glory. But this is the mystery of His love, that He receives the congregation of His believing people into a communion of good with Him, and makes them what He is—He the fulness of God, they the fulness of Christ, (1 Cor. iii. 23;) for so He is connected with them as the head with its body. By His vicarious death and resurrection He has become the head of His body, (Col. i. 18,) and from Him, as the head, the whole body, by joints and bands compacted and knit together into one, "increaseth with the increase of God," (Col. ii. 19; Eph. iv. 16.) The union of the sovereign Head with His subordinate members has its visible reflex in the matrimonial union of husband and wife, (Eph. v. 22, &c.) Yea, Paul joins head and members so intimately together into one whole, that of the body of the Church he says, "So also is *Christ*," (1 Cor. xii. 12,)—after the manner as the holy prophets call Christ the King of Israel, also simply "Israel," (cf. Isa. xlix. 3,)—and as what David sings, "I will give thanks unto Thee, O Lord, among the heathen, and sing praises unto Thy name," (Ps. xviii. 49,) is fulfilled in the Church of the Gospel, (Rom. xv. 9; cf. Acts xiii. 47.)

St Paul saw Jesus Christ in His heavenly glory. Wherein then consists the union of the head in heaven and the body on earth? He became conscious of this mystery when, at his baptism by Ananias, he was filled with the Holy Ghost. "He that is joined unto the Lord is one spirit" with Him, as the wife is one flesh with her husband. A temple of the Holy Ghost is the body of every believer, (1 Cor. vi. 17, &c.,) and God's temple are all believers together, because the Spirit of God dwelleth in them, (1 Cor. iii. 16; 2 Cor. vi. 16;) they—all that are in Christ Jesus—grow together unto an holy temple in the Lord: in whom they are also builded together for an habitation of God through the Spirit, (Eph. ii. 21-22.) Unity of the Spirit is the unity of the members, both with their Head and with one another, (Eph. iv. 3;) for the presence of the Lord in His Church is the presence of the Spirit, (2 Cor. iii. 17.) But as Paul himself received not the Holy Ghost without outward means, nor was otherwise kept by Him with Christ in the one true faith, but in the Church, in which the Spirit dwells and works; so he also now teaches that the Lord both effects and preserves the organic life of the body with its head by means of "joints and bands," ministering nourishment to it. How thoroughly far "the man of faith" and of the Spirit was from all fanaticism we have already seen, when viewing him in that character, (cf. Chap. VII.) Whereupon, then, does he ground the bridal dignity of the Church? Answer: "Christ loved the Church, and gave Himself for it; that He might sanctify and cleanse it with the washing of water by the word, that He might present it to Himself a glorious Church," (Eph. v. 25-27.) But whereby is the body of Christ built? By the Spirit are we all baptized into one body, whether we be Jews or Gentiles, whether we be bond or free; and have been all made to drink into one Spirit, (1 Cor. xii. 13; cf. the Old Test. figure of this in 1 Cor. x. 1-4.) In fine, he that receives the Spirit, receives Him "by the hearing of faith," (Gal. iii. 2.) It is the gracious work of the Spirit, in the audible word of preaching and the visible word of the sacrament, which begets and nourishes the Church, affiances her to Christ, and presents her to Him in bridal glory.

In his circular epistle to the congregations in Ephesus and around it, wherein Paul more especially unfolds the mystery of the Church, at the building up and bodily exhibition of which in the whole world he labours, we read in the fourth chapter how "the edifying of the body of Christ" is accomplished by Christ's Spirit through the Word and Sacrament. He that ascended up far above all heavens, that He might fill all things with His divinely-human glory, does by His grace make Himself palpably manifest in His Church on earth by means of the word of grace administered in His name by ministers of the Word. "And He gave some apostles, and some prophets, and some evangelists, and some pastors and teachers, for the perfecting of the saints, for the work of the ministry, for the edifying of the body of Christ." Who could have borne richer testimony to these gifts which the risen and ascended Saviour "gave unto men" than the Apostle Paul, who was himself a right royal gift from the immediate hand of royalty? Yet, deeply penetrated as he was with the peculiar costliness of the apostolic office intrusted to him "for obedience to the faith among all nations," (Rom. i. 5, xvi. 25, 26,) we, nevertheless, find him ever intent on emphasising and giving prominence to the essential unity of the "ministry of the New Testament," the "ministry of the Spirit," (2 Cor. iii.,) and the "ministry of reconciliation," (2 Cor. v. 18.) Therefore, also, he loves best to speak by "*we*" and "*us*," where he speaks of the office of "ministers" (under-workmen) "of Christ and stewards of the mysteries of God," (1 Cor. iv. 1;) therefore, too, he associates his name in the introductory salutations of nearly all epistles with some of his colleagues—not only Timothy (often) and Silas (twice), but also his humble brother Sosthenes, (1 Cor. i. 1;) therefore he says, (2 Cor. v. 20,) "we are ambassadors for Christ," and thus colleagues himself with all other "messengers," like Peter and John with their elders, (1 Pet. v. 1; 2 and 3 John i.) "There are diversities of gifts, but the same Spirit; and there are differences of administrations, but the same Lord," (1 Cor. xii. 4, 5,) Jesus Christ, who in the apostolic office, to which He has called him, as well as the twelve, has planted the root to all offices in the Church, whereby and wherein the Holy Ghost works with His manifold gifts "to the edifying of the body of Christ." As in the manifold branches of a tree one and the same tree is exhibited, so in the various ministerial offices one and the same ministry, ordained and instituted by Christ for His Church, and therefore of Divine mandate and right, though in its historical development, after human right and ecclesiastical order, it is *so, as it is*. In the passage already quoted (Eph. iv.) the Apostle dissects the ministerial office into several *distinct functions;* for what he means to say is, that the "*manifold gifts and* differences of administration of the one Lord" do not hinder but further the unity of the Church, ("unto every one of us is given grace, according to the measure of the gift of Christ;") but forthwith he comprehends again apostles, prophets, evangelists, pastors, and teachers, as all set for "the work of the ministry," whose every object and end is the same, the "perfecting of the saints," the "edifying of the body of Christ." The parallel passage to this (1 Cor. xii. 28) presents us the same blessed tree, as it shoots forth from the apostolic root into its various branches of gifts and offices. "God hath set some in the Church, first, apostles; secondarily, prophets; thirdly, teachers; after that miracles; then gifts of healings, helps, governments," (*i. e.*, working and administrative talents and operations,) "diversities of tongues." The apostles, and pre-eminently Paul, stood there in the fulness of all gifts, wherewith the Holy Ghost furnishes and adorns the Church, and we see them executing the "whole work of the ministry," for the which, in their several capacities, prophets, evangelists, pastors, teachers, and other office-bearers are appointed. Thus— as being primarily ordained for "the ministry of the word," (Acts vi. 4,) called and gifted for the guidance of the entire service done in and through the word of the Gospel to the edifying of the Church—the apostles are, to borrow a current phrase, the "princes of the Church;" and set as princes indeed they are to the Church of all times, for their word is the fountain of all evangelical preaching; and by it shall be judged, not only the twelve tribes of Israel, but we also, and all Gentiles. And this princely office and prerogative is theirs exclusively. "Built upon the foundation of the apostles and prophets," the whole building (of the Church) fitly framed together, rests upon Jesus Christ as the "chief corner-stone," upon whom the apostles were grounded first, (Eph. ii. 20.) But their followers in the ministry are all that are ordained to officiate in the Church, provided it be the Apostolic Word which they minister. The Lord continues the work He has begun, and in the way He began it, when appointing the firstfruits of His Church to be the first to minister in it, breathing on them with the Spirit of His mouth, in order that, by their word, filled with the Spirit, they might dispense the Church's treasures, foremost of which stands the forgiveness of sins to believers in Christ's name, while by the same word they are retained to unbelievers for judgment; whereunto Christ came into the world, (John xx. 21-23, ix. 39, xii. 47.) Therefore we have found Paul not only active in the ministry of the word, but have also seen him deem it part of his office to "ordain them elders in every church," (Acts xiv. 23,) of and to whom he says, "The Holy Ghost hath made you overseers to feed the Church of God," (Acts xx. 28.) In his very first epistle he writes,— "We beseech you, brethren, to know them which labour among you, and are over you in the Lord, and admonish you; and to esteem them very highly for their work's sake," (1 Thess. v. 12, 13.) And that the Apostle looks upon all elders (overseers, evangelists, pastors, and teachers) as his colleagues, we may see from his farewell address at Miletus, which is throughout an exhortation to the elders at Ephesus to follow their fellow-elder Paul.

"Ministry" and "diaconate" mean "service;" and so, in

fact, does "liturgy." It is Paul's comfort, as well as boast, that he holds his ministry from the Lord Himself. A "liturgus" of Jesus Christ he calls himself, commissioned and empowered to dispense the Gospel, (Rom. xv. 16.) Notwithstanding, he accepts the Lord's commission (1 Tim. i. 1) altogether in the sense of ministering love, and desires his office to be looked upon as a service which Christ, the great "Arch-deacon," (Jesus Christ was a "minister of the circumcision," Rom. xv. 8,) renders to the Church through His ministering servants, (1 Tim. iv. 6.) "We preach not ourselves, but Christ Jesus the Lord; and ourselves your servants for Jesus' sake," (2 Cor. iv. 5.) In love's service, he is devoted to his brethren for Christ's sake, in order that He alone—through the service done by commission under Him, and on His part— might be the Lord of all—a Lord who is among His servants, "as he that serveth," (Luke xxii. 27; John xiii. 16.) A labourer together with God he is in God's husbandry, (1 Cor. iii. 9,) who beseeches by him, (2 Cor. v. 20.) Wherefore he says,—"Not for that we have dominion over your faith, but are helpers of your joy," (2 Cor. i. 24;) for God lords none by imperious rule.into the joy of faith, but courts men into it by the gentle intreaty of His word of grace; and they that receive it shall reign in God— serving in liberty, themselves lorded by none, but led by the Spirit of joy, nourished and increased in them by the "helpers of their joy," and preserved to them, under God, by them that "watch for their souls," (Heb. xiii. 17.) " Who, then, is Paul, and who is Apollos, but ministers by whom ye believed, even as the Lord gave to every man?" (1 Cor. iii. 5.)

The Lord has ordained the ministry to serve *in* the Church, not to stand *between* Him and the Church. They (the ministers) do not float in the air, but are members and integral parts of the Church. No trace or thought of the office-bearers in the Church holding a mediatorial position between God and the Church can be found in Paul's epistles, or any place of the New Testament. In the three cardinal passages (Rom. xii.; 1 Cor. xiii., and Eph. iv.) where the Apostle treats of the different Church offices for the edifying of the body of Christ, he speaks of the gifts of the Lord, or the Spirit, as given to the Church, as an organic whole, to make use of them by persons whom she calls and sets apart to serve her with the received gifts. And these are made effectual by the Lord's command, and under His gracious operation, in the ministry, or "ministration of the Spirit," (2 Cor. iii. 8; Gal. iii. 5;) which, according to the necessities of the Church, is unfolded in different offices. In so far " the work of the ministry" in the Church emanates from her Head. But the persons divinely designated by their gifts for the ministry, and called unto it by the Church, are no "vicars of Christ," no proxies, no substitutes or representatives of the Head; but among the members of Christ's body is their place, those members whom God hath set severally, according to His will, to care for and serve one another in love.

For the Church is the body of Christ, in her capacity as the congregation of believers who, through the Holy Ghost, are gathered together under their Head, Christ; and for that reason they are united among one another in love, (Eph. iv. 16.) The Church is not constituted of a number of individuals, who form themselves into an association for their spiritual benefit, and keep together so long as it pleases them; but the Church is a family, the family of "the household of God," (Eph. ii. 19,) all begotten by His Spirit, and related by one blood of generation. "All" are "one in Christ Jesus," (Gal. iii. 28.) We have seen in Paul "the man of faith," to whom especially was communicated the mystery of the incorporation of the Gentiles into "the same body," (Eph. iii. 6;) the "labourer together with God," who devoted his whole life to carrying into effect, throughout the world, what Christ had shed His precious blood for,—the oneness of Jew and Gentile, the making "one new man" out of twain, (Eph. ii. 15,) the consummation of the true Israel of God. We have seen—to speak with Gregory of Nazianzum—"the herald of the Gentiles, who is a captain of the Jews." As Christ is both the substance of Paul's faith and sum-total of all his preaching, so the "fulness of Christ"—the Church—is the fulness of his evangelical doctrine. There is no trace in his apostolical teaching that does not bear, more or less directly, on the mystery of "Christ and the Church." Reconciliation and redemption, justification and life, present liberty in the Spirit and future glory, all the articles of Christian faith and hope, coincide and meet together in this one,—the apostolic doctrine of the body whose Head is Christ. Then only do we rightly understand the man of love when we understand the love wherein he walked as one which finds her object and consummation in the Church. "Edification" is everywhere the end of the love he exercises, and bids others to exercise, in the name of the Lord. To unity in the Spirit, to oneness in confession, to peace in life, he continually exhorts and stretches forward with all his might. The kingdom of God is righteousness and peace and joy in the Holy Ghost; but where this spiritual kingdom is established by faith, it manifests itself in love, which has regard to even such outward things as eating and drinking, and walks after this rule; "Let us therefore follow after the things which make for peace, and things wherewith one may edify another," (Rom. xiv. 17-19.) Here is the place where we have to view Paul as deputy of the Antiochian church to the synod at Jerusalem, (Acts xv.)

This journey of Paul to Jerusalem was one of love to the Church; whereunto the Lord, as has been already observed, strengthened him by a special revelation, (Gal. ii. 2;) and indeed he needed such strengthening. For was he not jeopardising his apostolical independence by taking the appearance upon him as if he subjected his gospel-preaching to the judgment of the first-called apostles? Would it not be construed into a tacit admission of their superiority to him? (Gal. ii. 6.) Did he not furnish the followers of "Cephas," who deemed him and his fellow-Apostles of the Circumcision superior to the after-called Apostle of the Gentiles, with weapons, by allowing himself to be ruled by their advice in any matter of Christian doctrine, life, and order? Surely, had Paul held himself for wise, he had not gone up to Jerusalem, or had there taken another position than we find he did. But Paul was lighted on this church-journey by the word: "That speaking the truth in love, we may grow up into Him in all things, which is the Head, even Christ," (Eph. iv. 15.) An Antiochian church had just witnessed the accession of four Gentile churches gathered by Paul and Barnabas, and had rejoiced with them that the Lord had "opened the door of faith unto the Gentiles," (Acts xiv. 27.) But in the Mother-Church at Jerusalem and in Judæa this joy over Paul's blessed draught was of a mixed character. The Apostles themselves, and those like-minded with them, would indeed be glad to find Peter's signally gracious entrance into Cornelius' house so richly confirmed by these "wonderful works of God." But not all were like-minded with Peter, and John, and James, the Lord's brother. Some Judaising Christians would hold their leaven of legal Pharisaic pride concealed under the cloak of Jewish patriotism and an attachment to Israel's honoured rights and "customs," (Acts xxi. 21;) and therefore wished to see circumcision and the observance of the law required of the Gentile Christians as necessary to salvation besides their faith in Jesus Christ. The Church's treasure, the truth of the Gospel, the only apostolic answer to the question: "Is Jesus Christ enough for justification and the forgiveness of sins to every man that believeth in Him?" was here at stake. Thanks be to God! the holy synod, "apostles and elders," which "came together for to consider this matter," were unanimous in the confession, to which the Holy Ghost gave utterance by Peter's mouth: "We believe, that through the grace of the Lord Jesus Christ we shall be saved, even as they" (of the Gentiles.) Now Paul and Barnabas could relate to the "silent" multitude that God, through them, had indeed wrought among the Gentiles what Peter had said—viz., that He had "purified their hearts by faith;" and James elucidated and confirmed by the prophetic word the acceptance of the Gentiles as the work of God. The three pillars, Peter, James, and John, found Paul's gospel-edifice among the heathen needful of no propping up by additional doctrines, and gave Paul and Barnabas—over the one and only Gospel—" the right hands of fellowship," (Gal. ii. 6-9.) They were unanimous in disowning and rejecting as slanderous the sinister reports whereby false brethren from Judæa had disturbed the church at Antioch; and thus these peace-disturbers were happily foiled and beaten. The holy synod, however, being gathered in the spirit of truth and love, did more than merely acknowledge the Christian liberty of the Gentile churches. They also deemed it their duty to furnish them with helps for the maintenance of a laudable Christian order of life. The ordinances of the Jewish law, still observed by the Christians gathered from among the Jews, were not fitting barriers of church order for the Gentile churches, inasmuch as they had not first to become Jews in order to become Christians as fully as those. The synod, therefore, upon the advice of James, supplied them with certain rules for the fixing of a wise discipline and fair Christian order in the spirit of love, and resolved to write to them "that they should abstain from pollutions of idols," (especially from "things offered unto idols," 1 Cor. viii.,) "and from fornication," (all and every lawlessness in the sexual relations of life, 1 Cor. vi. 18; Gal. v. 19; Eph. v. 3; Col. iii. 5; 1 Thess. iv. 3,) "and from things strangled, and from blood," (Gen. ix. 4; Deut. xii. 23.) By this the communal life of the young Gentile churches was hedged in with a barrier of laudable caution against all impure and obscene heathen practices; while, by the last precept, a tender regard also was shewn to their Jewish brethren. "It seemed good to the Holy Ghost, and to us," it says in the body of the synodal letter, "to lay upon you no greater burden than these necessary things." What! Did not Paul protest against such a resolution? Did he lend himself to imposing upon churches of his gathering and building up synodal precepts as enacted by the Holy Ghost; and that, too, such as had regard to mere externals—to "meat" and drink?" And was he going to "subject" them again to such "ordinances?" (Col. ii. 20–22.) Yet Luke has not omitted expressly to mention that Paul, upon his next visitation-journey through the churches of Asia Minor, delivered them the "decrees" for "to keep" that were ordained of the apostles and elders at Jerusalem; yea, and he adds, what now-a-days may sound strange and even vexatious to some people, "and so were the churches established in the faith, and increased in number daily," (Acts xvi. 4, 5.) Thus, then, Paul must have deemed the holy synod to have written aright: "It seemed good to the Holy Ghost, and to us;" and he held thus of it because he found in the synod's decree only an explanatory copy of one and the same *law of love*, which Christ puts in the hearts of His believing people, and which the Holy Ghost establishes and keeps up in the Church.

Exactly so, as here at the synod in Jerusalem, we find Paul minded everywhere. With all diligence, as a good ruler, (Rom. xii. 18,) he upheld the maintenance of unity in the Church: "Endeavour to keep the unity of the Spirit in the bond of peace," (Eph. iv. 3.) In this passage the two things are paired together, which in the synodal decree also go hand in hand: unity in the spirit of faith, preserved by the Spirit of love in the bond of peace. "There is one body and one Spirit," he continues, (Eph. v. 4-6), "even as ye are called in one hope of your calling; one Lord, one faith, one baptism, one God and Father of all, who is above all, and through all, and in you all." He wants Christians to feel themselves as one integral and indivisible body, even as the Spirit is one and indivisible, who, through the Gospel, calls and gathers all in one hope of the same calling. One Lord is the Lord of them all, and therefore the faith of them all can be but one; and one baptism admits and makes them all His own. One God and Father it is whom all His children in Christ call "Abba, Father!" by the spirit of adoption. He is God over them all as their Creator, through them all as their Preserver, in them all as their Guide and Director. As Paul thankfully appeals to the "true" God that his and his fellow-labourers' preaching of the one Lord Jesus Christ has not been "yea and nay," (2 Cor. i. 18)—otherwise the Church of the living God were not the "pillar and ground of the truth," (1 Tim. iii. 15,) but a spurious counter or a weathercock—so we find him exhorting his congregations everywhere to be of one mind in Christ, (Rom. xv. 5, 6; Phil. ii. 2.) He saw their concord in sound doctrine already endangered, if they did not hold fast " the form of sound words" delivered by the apostles, (2 Tim. 1, 13.) " Now I beseech you, brethren, by the name of our Lord Jesus Christ, that ye all speak the same thing, and that there be no divisions among you; but that ye be perfectly joined together in the same mind and in the same judgment," (1 Cor. i. 10.) But oneness in faith and unity in doctrine have to be supported by their own offspring, concord and love. With parental fondness the Apostle paints before the Corinthians the many-membered body of the Church, so manifoldly-gifted by the self-same Spirit, (1 Cor. xii.), "For as the body is one, and hath many members, and all the members of that one body, being many, are one body; so also is Christ. For by one Spirit are we all baptized into one body, whether we be Jews or Gentiles, whether we be bond or free; and have been all made to drink into one Spirit. For the body is not one member, but many. If the foot shall say, Because I am not the hand, I am not of the body; is it therefore not of the body? And if the ear shall say, Because I am not the eye, I am not of the body; is it therefore not of the body? If the whole body were an eye, where were the hearing? If the whole were hearing, where were the smelling? But now hath God set the members every one of them in the body, as it hath pleased Him." The congregation at Corinth, and each individual congregation, is to consider itself as such a body, the manifold members of which need one another, and therefore must care for one another. Yet it is not Paul's meaning that, for instance, the congregation at Corinth or that at Rome do each form one body without any organic connexion between them. Bidding grace and peace unto the church of God which is at

Corinth, he adds: "To them that are sanctified in Christ Jesus, called to be saints, with all that *in every place* call upon the name of Jesus Christ our Lord, both theirs and ours," (1 Cor. i. 2;) thus deeming every place his own that holds any of them. Likewise he writes to the Romans: "As we have many members in one body, and all members have not the same office: so we, being many, are one body in Christ, and every one members one of another. Having then gifts, differing according to the grace that is given to us, whether prophecy, let us prophesy according to the proportion of faith; or ministry, let us wait on our ministering; or he that teacheth, on teaching," (Rom. xii. 4-7.) Yea, so studiously did the man who had upon him "the care of all the churches" (2 Cor. xi. 28) foster the spirit of true catholicity, that, in the Corinthians' "ministration" to the saints at Jerusalem he recognises a distribution "unto *all*," (2 Cor. ix. 13.) Verily Paul was no fanatic, nor a "Congregationalist," or "Independent." In his "we, being many, are one body in Christ," he includes all who belong and hold themselves to the "little flock" gathered around the Gospel, and ranged under the banners of Christ's Cross, whether at Rome, or Corinth, from Jerusalem even unto the ends of the earth. Well indeed he knows that only true believers are "one body in Christ," of whom He is the Head; yet he knows nothing of a body or church so spiritual and invisible that he might be unable to find or reach them with his apostolic exhortation. Are there among those, of whom he says "we, being many, are one body in Christ," some or many who do not believe in their heart what they confess with their mouth, and do not therefore cleave to the invisible Head, while, like Judas, they move among the visible members of the body? Well, in them the spiritual and invisible Church is not represented; though they are in the Church or body, they are not of the Church or body of Christ; they are the rubbish among the vessels of Christ—dead members among the living—withered branches among the green. Nor does the existence of such "vessels unto dishonour" subvert the "pillar and ground of the truth;" for the foundation of God standeth sure, having this seal : "The Lord knoweth them that are His," yesterday, and to-day, and for ever, (Num. xvi. 5;) and His own are to remain steadfast in the doing of the word : "Let every one that nameth the name of Christ depart from iniquity," (2 Tim. ii. 19-21.) For where persons who call themselves Christians make themselves known by their works as un-Christians and Anti-christians, neither will be checked by brotherly discipline, there Paul commands : "Put away from among you that wicked person," (1 Cor. v. 13.) But the melancholy fact, of which he was fully aware, that in this life "there are (and always will be) many false Christians and hypocrites, yea, and open sinners too, among the true believers," did not by any means determine him to fix the Christian Church, which "properly is nothing but the congregation of all believers and saints," into the open air of a mere idea, stripping her of her organic palpability, as subsisting in the preached and confessed Christ, and to dream of an invisible Church beside and out of the visible. "I say to every man that is among you," he writes to the Roman Church, (Rom. xii. 3; cf. 1 Cor. xii. 27: "Now ye are the body of Christ, and members in particular;") and with that at Rome he comprehends into one all churches of Christ in all places; for "so we," he says, "being many, are one body in Christ." A glance into the church-building and church-ruling activity of the Apostle shews plainly enough that he meant the picture he has drawn in 1 Cor. xii. of the body with many members, as valid for the collection of all individual congregations.

From the very first (cf., for instance, Acts xvi. 3) we find him employed to connect in the bond of peace the different new congregations springing up here and there, and by living joints to strengthen the tender bands of the several individual congregations into one whole. The identical name of "church," which not only each congregation, but even a small fraction of one, (Rom. xvi. 5; 1 Cor. xvi. 9,) bears together with the collective whole—*ecclesia*—already clearly points to this, that, according to apostolic doctrine and practice, the Christians scattered sectionally through the world constitute one organic whole, the parts of which grow together, and stand in service-rendering relation to one another. The heavenly organism of the Church consists in the union of many in one Spirit and faith, wrought by the means of grace; but this inward union manifests itself in outward signs, and is nourished and preserved by visible means. Paul desires the saints' "perfection," complete restoration—*Katartisis*, (2 Cor. xiii. 9;) and this he sees grow out of their close union (1 Cor. i. 10) and organic edification, (Eph. iv. 12, 13,) as one community or congregation of the Lord. Unto the giving and receiving of "spiritual" and "carnal" things (Rom. xv. 27) the several Christians and Christian congregations are joined together in love; for God is love, and His Church is the visible embodiment of love, (cf. 1 John iv. 12.) It is God's will that the several members of the body shall need one another, care for one another, and allow themselves to be cared for one by the other; therefore He has manifoldly distributed the manifold gifts of the one Spirit among the several members of the undivided, and every division-resisting, body, and points them mutually to each other's edification. Be it prophecy or ministry, teaching or exhortation; be it ruling and guiding, or the dispensing of bodily benefits, such as care for the sick and poor, with all other exercises of mercy, (Rom. xii. 6-8)—every gift of grace is given to each for the whole ; and Paul, the "ruler," best, shews how that gift (*Kybernesis*, art of steering, 1 Cor. xii. 28) has to be made effective in serving the whole body to edification, by discerning and awakening, commissioning and installing, watching over and applying, the manifold gifts to the general good of the Church, according to circumstances of place and time. The common gift of all Christians, Prayer—as if proceeding from the one heart in the body—Paul stirs continually into hearty motion and vigorous exercise by his constant exhortations to Intercession. As, to his great comfort, he knows himself borne up by the prayers of the Church, (2 Cor. i. 11 ; Phil. i. 19; Philemon 22,) and urgently commends himself to them, (Rom. xv. 30 ; Eph. vi. 19 ; Col. iv. 3 ; 1 Thess. v. 15;) so he seeks to increase the union of all saints, here and there, by exhorting them to intercessions and thanksgiving for each other, (Eph. vi. 18,) and for all men, (1 Tim. ii. 1.) The singing of God's praise by all brethren, with one mind and one mouth, (Rom. xv. 6,) was to him the holy bloom of church-life, pregnant with much fruit, of which it has the promise. The uniform Latin tongue kept up in the Romish Church, although lapsed into the service of perversion, is one of Claudius' "beacons at sea, to indicate that a richly-laden vessel has suffered shipwreck there." In all respects the "man of the Church" proved himself a faithful guardian and diligent fosterer of the precious organic union and communion whereto all Christians scattered over the whole earth are called. An instance of his fond solicitude in this direction we have seen in the collection he gathered with such painstaking diligence, cementing thereby in one bond of peaceful union the saints in Judæa and those of his several Gentile congregations.

Our attention has already been drawn to that memorable

passage in 1 Cor. xiv., (cf. p. 160,) where, of his directions for decent order in the church service, the Apostle says: "The things that I write unto you are the commandments of the Lord," (1 Cor. xiv. 37.) By this we are not to understand as though the several precepts he there gives were communicated to him by special revelation, (cf. 1 Cor. vii. 12-25,) but rather as he himself explains his meaning to this effect: "For God is not the author of confusion, but of peace." As "all churches of the saints," so the one at Corinth has to shew itself as a congregation of the God of peace and order. "Let all things be done decently and in order." In drawing into the sphere of his apostolical management and control all such things as the manner of Divine service and church discipline, (yea, and even customs, to the very wearing of woman's hair,) matrimonial order, and the administration of the poor-box—in short, all that is comprehended under the term of "church order"—"So ordain I in all churches," (1 Cor. vii. 17;) "the rest will I set in order when I come," (1 Cor. xi. 34)—and claiming for these regulations the church's obedience, as one due to the Lord, the Apostle is far from putting a yoke upon the neck of the disciples, and of bringing the happily freed Christian souls again from evangelical liberty under legal restraints. He is plain, indeed, where church order and discipline is concerned, (1 Cor. v. 11,) and can boldly write "I will therefore," both as regards matters of Christian duty as well as Christian decency, (1 Tim. ii. 8, &c.;) yea, and "command" he can, "in the name of our Lord Jesus Christ, that ye withdraw yourselves from every brother that walketh disorderly, and not after the traditions which he received of us," (2 Thess. iii. 6;) and, "but if any man," he can peremptorily say, "seem to be contentious, we have no such custom, neither the churches of God," (1 Cor. xi. 16.) Yet what are all the orders according to which he desires the Christian Church to walk, but copies and precepts of edifying love, resulting from faith? They are enforced by no "staff of the driver," except it be that of Him who "driveth"* God's children; and their love is not ignorant of it, (cf. 1 Cor. xiv. 38,) but understands the Spirit's voice. And because church precepts do but regulate works of love, they are not immutable; for love alters her works according to time and circumstances, place and persons—"adapt yourselves to the time."† But Paul's sense is caught as little as Luther's,‡ if their names are made use of for justifying an evangelical liberty which wants to be free from, and independent of, that general order whereby the one body is served and edified by all its constituent parts. The "Congregational system," for instance, loses sight of this important point in not viewing the Church as one *organic* whole. That only can change which exists. As the living human body constantly changes in its growth, yet always remains the same human body, and never becomes a spectre; exactly so does the changeableness of church order not consist in this, that possibly there might be no order at all, but in its changing according to its own

---

* Luther's forcible rendering of ἄγω in Rom. viii. 14.

† Luther's translation of two different passages—Rom. xii. 11, and Eph. v. 16. In the former he must have followed quite another reading (than τῷ Κυρίῳ δουλεύοντες,) and in the latter have been swayed by the context; for the English, here also, is decidedly the correcter rendering (of ἐξαγοράζομαι.)—Tr.

‡ Luther, for instance, in speaking of the Saxon-church-visitation-order, says: "From which common order to deviate creates no good thoughts, and eventually even disruption and devastation of the Church. We should thank God that our churches are brought a little into uniform order; and God will not bless them who, without any need, only for their own ambition and pride, break in upon such order and unity. But may God be our help and strength in the maintenance of a true faith and unfeigned love! Amen." Such like things, therefore, are really "old," and not "new Lutheran."

inherent law : " Let all your things be done with charity," (1 Cor. xvi. 14;) and again, " Edify one another," (1 Thess. v. 11.)

In conclusion, we shall take a view of the three (so-called) " pastoral letters." They faithfully reflect the picture of Paul, as a clever pilot steering the vessel of Christ. Pastoral letters we call the two Epistles to Timothy and the one to Titus, because they are written to pastors, and mainly treat of how they ought to be, and how they ought to execute their office. They might, however, as properly be called letters on church government; for the church "ruler" writes them to his two assistants, ("apostolical vicars" they have been not unaptly called,) that they might know how to "set in order" the things wanting, as he had appointed them, (Tit. i. 5.) A "superintendental instruction" they contain, (for "superintendents" of Ephesus and Crete respectively Timothy and Titus have also been styled, by our fathers,) inasmuch as the pastoral and other instructions therein given are meant to serve them as a norm for the management of church affairs, which, for instance, is pointedly expressed in injunctions like these : " Let no widow be taken into the number under threescore years," (1 Tim. v. 9), and "let the elders that rule well be counted worthy of double honour; (ib. ver. 17.) Now, how were Timothy and Titus to " behave themselves in the house of God?" (1 Tim. iii. 15.) First, and chief, stands the care in keeping incorrupt the only true doctrine, and watching over it that it be so kept. Paul's First Epistle to Timothy at once begins by mentioning why he had left his "own son in the faith" at Ephesus—viz., that he might " charge some that they teach no other doctrine." Strange doctrine, or rather strange teaching, (heterodidaskaly,) he is not to suffer. The spirit of error and heresy did not yet venture, it would appear, to come out boldly with a denial of the apostolic doctrine; but some, satiated with the plain Christian food, "gave heed to fables and endless genealogies," and were "doting about questions and strifes of words." Against these Paul binds upon Timothy's conscience the two cardinal articles for Christian edification—faith and love,—and calls to his mind " the glorious Gospel of the blessed God," which was committed to his trust. "This charge I commit unto thee, son Timothy," he most solemnly writes him, and exhorts the watchman over the house of God to "war a good warfare." Prominent among all his injunctions regarding the Christian life in the Church stands always the heeding of a sound faith and teaching, as the chief charge of his office, (1 Tim. vi. 12-14 ;) and at the close of this epistle he once more calls out to him: " O Timothy, keep that which is committed to thy trust, avoiding profane and vain babblings, and oppositions of science falsely so called, which some professing have erred concerning the faith." His main charge upon Titus, likewise, is to ordain such elders and bishops "in every city" as, like "faithful stewards of God," shall uphold the word of " sound doctrine," and contrariwise to "stop the mouth" of those who "for filthy lucre's sake teach things which they ought not," tickling the Cretans' lie-accustomed ears with "Jewish fables and commandments of men." As a " pattern of good works" he ought always to shew himself, but withal to watch over "uncorruptness in doctrine," (Tit. ii. 7;) the sweetest kernel of which is contained in the two Christmas epistles (Tit. ii. 11-14, and iii. 4-7); to which severally the Apostle adds: "These things speak and exhort, and rebuke with all authority. Let no man despise thee;" "This is a faithful saying, and these things I will that thou affirm constantly." The Second Epistle to Timothy contains Paul's last will and testament to his "dearly beloved son." Once more "Paul the aged" lays his blessing hand upon him, encouraging his sorrowful disciple (2 Tim. i. 4) to " stir up the gift of God, which" (he says) "is in thee by the putting on of my hands," (ib. ver. 6;) and here also his main exhortation is still, "Hold fast the form of sound words, which thou hast heard of me, in faith and love which is in Christ Jesus. That good thing which was committed unto thee keep by the Holy Ghost which dwelleth in us," (ib. ver. 13, 14.) The more boldly and shamelessly the Antichristian spirits are throwing off their mask, bent on committing havoc in the "house of God," the more bravely and courageously Timothy is to put on his strength in Christ, fully confiding in the Lord, who will give him understanding rightly (without addition or omission) to divide the word of truth, and to "purge himself" from all seducers, who are growing worse and worse. "But watch thou in all things, endure afflictions, do the work of an evangelist, make full proof of thy ministry," (2 Tim. iv. 5.) Grounded upon this passage in particular, some have latterly thought the office of an "evangelist" to be virtually the same with the "episcopate;" so that Timothy, even in his character as evangelist, had been "bishop" of Ephesus, in the sense of ecclesiastical rule, which it can be proved has been attached to that official title since the second century.* Though this assumption goes too great a length, ("evangelists" are all preachers of the Gospel among the heathen; for instance "Philip the evangelist," Acts xxi. 8,) yet so much is quite plain, that Timothy the "evangelist" was to fulfil (*i.e.*, *fully* execute) his office, not alone by preaching the Gospel, teaching and exhorting, (to which, however, he certainly was to give continual attendance, 1 Tim. iv. 13; 2 Tim. iv. 2;) but also thereby, that —as the apostle's legate—he exercised the same ruling

* Thus Lechler: Die neutestamentliche Lehre vom heiligen Amte.— P. 220, &c.

and administrative functions which we see Paul himself do :—To him, as well as Titus, was committed the care to see that in their respective dioceses the preaching of the Gospel be carried on by truly evangelical men, and that their congregations be edified in a manner becoming the Gospel of Christ. To this end they had to look out for and choose well-qualified persons, to instruct, to examine, and to ordain them for their several offices, by the laying on of hands (1 Tim. iii. 1, &c., v. 9, &c., ver. 22 ; 2 Tim. ii. 2 ; Tit. i. 5, &c.) Over the deacons and elders, (bishops,) both them that preached and those doing other evangelical service in the Church, they had the superintendence, to uphold the respect of their office, and provide for their maintenance, (1 Tim. v. 17-18;) but also to watch over their doctrine and conversation, to receive accusations against them, yet guardedly and upon sufficient proof by witnesses, and to administer reproof or other condign correction, (jurisdiction;) but withal having the utmost care to "do nothing by partiality," (1 Tim. v. 19-21,) and after the rule : " Rebuke not an elder, but entreat him as a father; and the younger men as brethren; the elder women as mothers; the younger as sisters, with all purity," (1 Tim. v. 1, 2.) Finally, the entire church order was put under their supervision, both that of the manner of Divine service (1 Tim. ii.) and the discipline of the congregations in doctrine and life, (1 Tim. vi. 1, &c.; Tit. ii. 1, &c., iii. 1, &c.) To sum up all—the Apostle has drawn in these epistles the functions of a careful "ruler," such as Luther speaks of, on the words " he that ruleth, with diligence," (Rom. xii. 8 :) " They are those who are to watch over all offices in the Church ; that the teachers wait on teaching, and be not slothful, likewise the ministers on ministering, and be not dilatory, but do rightly dispense the treasure ; punish and excommunicate sinners, and have diligent care to see all functions faithfully exercised. Such are the bishops' functions; wherefore also they are called bishops or overseers, and 'antistites,' as St Paul calls them here—*i.e.*, prelates and rulers."

*Verba docent, exempla trahunt,* words teach, examples draw. If the Apostle has not taught us in express words that the Church ought at all times, in care for her organic edification, to call to the office of ruling overseers or administrators such men as the Holy Ghost has furnished with that gift, such at least must be our conviction, by the example he has drawn for us in Timothy and Titus.

But, above all, let us hold firm to St Paul's divine word and doctrine, that it may rule us as with the sceptre of the Lord! Tertullian beheld in Paul "little Benjamin," who rules where God is blest for* "the fountain of Israel," (Ps. lxviii. 26, 27.) Of such rule there will be no end " so long as the gathering around this fountain lasts." We have ventured to extol the merits of this prince among God's saints, not as if he needed "letters of commendation," who in all believers' hearts has a living letter of honour "known and read of all men," (2 Cor. iii. 1-3;) but because we are mindful of his exhortation: " Remember them which have the rule over you, who have spoken unto you the word of God; whose faith follow, considering the end of their conversation," (Heb. xiii. 7.) May this " portrait" of Paul, and his example, draw us to the obedience of the faith he once taught, is still teaching, and will teach to the end! Now and ever may the imperishable blessing rest on the Church, whereof Chrysostom spoke fourteen centuries back: " By his epistles Paul ever lives in every man's mouth throughout the world. Through them have been blessed not only the heathen congregations that were

* Luther's translation of the Hebrew (Septuagint: ἐκ πηγῶν) in Ps. lxviii. 26; instead of the English correct rendering: "from the foundation."—Tr.

gathered by him, but all believers down to this day; yea and will be blessed all saints still to be born till the coming of the Lord." Amen.

> Christ, champion of Thy Church, that war-worn host
> Who bear Thy cross, haste, help, or we are lost!
> The schemes of those who long our blood have sought
>     Bring Thou to nought.
>
> Do Thou Thyself for us Thy children fight,
> Withstand the devil, quell his rage and might;
> Whate'er assails Thy members left below
>     Do Thou o'erthrow.
>
> Raise men like Paul, both in our Church and School!
> Fill all with grace whom Thou dost raise to rule!
> Faith, hope, and love, O Christ, to every heart
>     Do Thou impart!
>
> So shall Thy goodness here be still adored,
> Thou guardian of Thy "little flock," dear Lord,
> And heaven and earth through all eternity
>     Shall worship Thee.

THE END.

www.ingramcontent.com/pod-product-compliance
Lightning Source LLC
Chambersburg PA
CBHW021844230426
43669CB00008B/1074